For My Grandchildren:

A Book of Wisdom

By Samuel J.M. Donnelly

PublishAmerica
Baltimore

ISBN: 978-1-60749-714-1
PUBLISHED BY PUBLISHAMERICA, LLLP
www.publishamerica.com
Baltimore

Printed in the United States of America

For the Lord Jesus
And my children and grandchildren
And may they get to know
Each other

Table of Contents

VOLUME I:
THE ETERNAL SHAPE CHANGER 9
VOLUME II:
THE JIGSAW PIECE 69
FINDING THE PRESENCE OF GOD, A CRITICAL
    AND EXPLANATORY ESSAY 174

Introduction

I wrote most of these poems between my 70th and 73rd birthdays in roughly the order presented. The poems are related to each other and are designed to be read together. I have grouped them into poems related in time and thought. A suggestion: Read Volume I straight through one evening and Volume II straight through the next night.

VOLUME I
THE ETERNAL SHAPE CHANGER

The Coming Autumn

The Paths of Life

How glorious in autumn
The forests of the east
Splendid in sunlight,
Orange, red and green,
Pines, oaks and maples
Blended together.

How splendid in springtime
The forests of the west,
Towering pine, Douglas firs,
Redwoods, sequoias,
The forest floor
Covered with ferns,
Wonderful to walk
The cool, mysterious paths.

I have walked the forest paths
In splendor and delight
I look forward to walking
The forests of heaven.

Yellow Leaves or None or Few

How beautiful to see the leaves fall,
Yellow leaves drifting down
Under the yellow tree,
Yellow tree standing majestically
Against a backdrop of pines
And maples, green, red and yellow.

From my picture window I see
The yellow leaves fall.
When our seasons of sun
Decline into fall
Will we be beautiful
Like the yellow leaves of autumn?
Will we float in the air
As we drift majestically down?

On My 70th Birthday: Laudate si mi Signore

Praise to You, my gracious Lord
For sunsets spread across the sky
For beauty ever splendid.
Praise to You, my gracious Lord
For constant love and rescue
For kindness and forgiveness
Praise to You, my gracious Lord
For teaching us Your ways
For joining in our journey
Praise to You, my gracious Lord
For friendship everlasting
Praise to You my gracious Lord
For seventy years of life, and
For Brother Francis and his inspiration.

The Eternal Shape Changer:
Reflections on Creation—12 poems

The Physical Universe

God's Glory in a Blade of Grass

White rooted spear of green
Heaven aimed like Gothic spire
Brush stroke on landscape earth
Major poet's minor work,
Pacing slowly up and down
Father Cox addressed the grass.
Pacing quickly up and down
Father Cox addressed the class.
See, look and you can find
God's glory in a blade of grass.

Waterfalls

Glory be to God for waterfalls
Cascading and laughing
On a sunny afternoon

Roaring and tumbling down the slopes,
Powerful and beautiful,
They mirror their creator
Like the gentle water
Which washes our faces.

Flashing and shining
Like light from shaken foil
They delight like the sunbeams
That dance on a lake

Clear and translucent
As I look at the crest
The water seems permanent
At the top of the fall

Action and permanence
Crash with a roar
That could be heard
In the silence
For thousands of years.

Beauty

Black and red amid the autumn color
Cardinals whistling through the yellow leaves
Crows on their early flight greeting all who hear
So I wake at morning to the calling of the birds.
Daylight starts with a message from the Lord,
Day after day, a wakeup call from God.

Fall colors luminous in twilight
Just before the sunset and as the sun goes down,
On the feeder sits the cardinal
Beauty beyond beauty for a moment in the evening.

Now the chickadee gives its lovesick call amid the February snow,
While the sun is rising in a cloudy sky.
The gleaming snow lies under a purple heaven touched with rose,
Beauty and the first signs of spring amid the deepest winter.

Sunlight's essential to the life of the world
Beauty's a grace gratuitously added,
Thoughtfully added for us to see.

Beauty bears witness to the presence of a person,
Beauty must communicate,
Beauty's interpersonal,
Person to person,
A message of love.

God Fathers Forth

How wonderful to transform
Monkeylike ancestors into men,
Giant tree towering dinosaurs
Or their relatives
Into singing birds.

Struggle by historic struggle
The kaleidoscope
Of mutating genes changes.
God fathers forth
The shape changing wonders
Of our dynamic world;
Sharp the vision that finds
The way to mold our DNA.

History tumbles, sometimes stumbles
Down the drama laden ages.
Men and women interweaving
Forge their destiny,
Driven by their visions,
Seeking larger visions,
Growing in understanding,
Knowledge, maybe love,
Person by struggling person,
Meeting other persons
Encountering changing nature
In the ordered chaos
Of a growing, changing world.

Systems

Imagine the earth
As a giant factory with many systems
Huge and interlocking
Doing its work,
Plate tectonics
Moving continental shelves
Over the mantle
Creating continents,
Altering their shape,
Clouds and wind and all
That constitutes climate,
Hurricanes, tornadoes,
Sometimes tropically hot
Then ice age cold
Revived to life by volcanoes.

Then picture an asteroid
Destroying life
Creating new possibilities
As did the continents
When they formed Pangaea
Destroying trilobites
Swimming in shallow seas
That were no more,
Preparing a platform
For dinosaurs to roam
With their long legs
And towering presence.

Now the genome,
The genetic system

Building bodies
And generations,
Preserving life,
Adapting, struggling,
Mutating randomly
Able to survive
When large is good
Or when small is necessary,
Here, too, is a system
Interlocking with climate,
Asteroids and plate tectonics.

The cardinal and the chimpanzee
Emerge from the interlocking systems
Not designed minutely,
Rather manufactured
By the systems
Which appear intelligently designed
To do exactly but not precisely
That.

Studying the Bang

Mathematical formulas dance
In the sky,
As waves from that early bang
Echo down the ages,
As on a spiral arm of
A disc like galaxy,
We trace the implications
Of that original event.

Scientific minds can grasp
The basic structure,
Use their analysis to predict
What they will find.

Like the poet seeing beauty
Scientific thinkers
Meet another mind.

Although some do deny it,
They see the great creator
Whose formulas underpin
The sparkling dancing stars.

Recognition

To enter the kingdom
You must enter as a child
Eyes full of wonder
Seeing what you see

Catching Eternal Beauty
In His echoes here,
Recognizing God
Like another Person
Recognizing Love
When He reaches out
His hand.

Like Elijah on the mountain
We catch a glimpse of God,
Simple recognition
Available to all,
To Galileo in the tower,
To the poor man raking leaves.

Galileo in the tower,
Archimedes running naked,
Symbols of discovery,
Joy at recognition,
Forging method, scientific method
While creating modern thought.

Let us celebrate the creators
Of modern methodology,
Mathematics, science, logic,
Adding economics,
Softer subjects too.

Clashing methods cloud our judgment,
Confusing vision, puzzling us,
Whirling through our minds,
Leaving clouds of dust.
We need to puzzle through
The foundations of our methods.
Where is Galileo?
Hey, we need him now.

To find the Creator (not analyze His works)
Requires simple insight,
The insight we use
When greeting a friend,
Interpreting his language
Knowing what he wants.

Insight acquired
Often after struggle
After thinking
Through our methods,
After struggling with our sins
Or the suffering in the world.

The Human Drama

The Drama of Life: Two Poems

I.
In green and brown my love went out to play among the leaves.
In brown and green my love sat down among the autumn leaves
Began a poem written for the woman I love.

"Who Who are you you? Are you you a who who?",
Began a poem I wrote for the children she bore.

"I'm tired," the poor man said.
"You know I get just as tired as you,"
He said, while raking my leaves.

The old woman labored with heavy breathing.
She died with her mouth open, struggling for breath.
She relaxed when I made a cross on her forehead,
A person in her final moments.

Every who who is a you you
Read the children's poem.
How do we participate in the life of another?
How do others participate in the drama of life?

II.
Here on a little planet
Circling the galaxy
Every two hundred and fifty million
Years or so

God created evolution and hence
The drama of life.

God created sex, man and woman
Interacting.
God created the struggle for morality,
The struggle for relation,
To live life well,
To be together.

God set the stage for human drama.
God set before us life and death
And said to us,
Choose life.

Wisdom

Once there was an old man skilled at making toys
So my children rode a rocking horse
And their children ride it too.

Once there was an old man who sat beneath a pine tree.
"Never let your right hand,"
I've heard him say,
Whenever giving charity
"Know about your left hand."
Wisdom grows with age,
The knowledge of the making,
The knowledge of relation,

The wisdom of an old man rocking in his chair
The wisdom of a fishing guide searching out his prey,
The wisdom of Odysseus sailing home from Troy,
The wisdom of Ben Sirach preaching to his son,
The wisdom of our God playing in the dawn, crafting His world.

Wisdom understands, it knows how to do.
Wisdom knows more than accumulating knowledge.
Wisdom's crafty, wisdom's creative
Wisdom like Solomon resolves human dilemmas.
Wisdom's good at relations and persons.
Wisdom understands the presence of God.

To Make Friendship Possible

Only God is perfect,
Only God is good.
With loving humility
He chooses to create
An evolving, developing
Imperfect world,
Allowing creatures room
To grow, repent and change.

Alone in majestic splendor
God creates a fireball
And starts electrons dancing
Knowing at the far end
There lies a Crucifixion
As He joins His suffering creatures
In the drama of their lives.

Thinking He'll make breakfast
Standing by the lakeshore
Before an open fire
Gathering His friends
With quiet affection
Following the drama
That shook their lives.

Blessing the wine
In the tradition of the ages
While He sits at dinner
Anticipating death
He remembers the fireball
And dancing in the dawn,

Preparation for the friendship
He offers His disciples.

Alone in the universe
God reaches out
To make friendship possible
To create the human drama
Where friend encounters friend
And God encounters us
Sharing in our suffering
In our less than perfect lives.
Only God is perfect.
He chooses imperfection
When He chooses to create.

Christmas

Shortly after midnight
On a Christmas morning
God entered our world
And was wrapped
In swaddling clothes.

While uttering a new Word
He changes creation,
The Eternal Shape Changer,
The Creative Word,
Structuring a new world
Quietly in a stable
While He rests on the straw.

By sharing our destiny
He changes that destiny,
The Eternal Shape Changer
Changing our lives,
Turning water into wine,
Offering us His friendship
By joining our journey.

"Behold," He says, "I make all things new."
"All manner of things, now shall be well."
The Creator of imperfection
Shares our imperfection,
While making the poorest
His brothers and sisters.

Easter

Tears are not the final word.
Though the Roman poet sang
Exclaiming tears are at the heart of things,
Tears are not the final word.

The Word of God is speaking from the Cross
Tears are not the final word.
In this bloody suffering world
Tears are not the final word
Because the Word of God
Is speaking from the Cross.

Praise to You my Gracious Lord
In this bloody suffering world
For speaking from the Cross
That tears are not the final word.

Autumn:
A Fall Quartet Plus One

1. Fall Begins

Early evening and the blue jays
Are having a shouting match
Calling each other thief.
Remains of the sunset float
On the rim of the sky.
Across the sky
The moon is rising.

A sign of early fall:
In the neighborhood some branches
Are turning orange, red and yellow
The beginning of the blazing beauty
Of Fall.

2. A Ride in the Country

In this first week of October
Not yet the blazing beauty of fall
But as I turned the car
Toward the Pompey hills
And on to Fabius
And beyond yet deeper in the country
I saw crows on cornstalks
Cut close to the ground,

Red leaves on sumac,
The first in the fall,
Orange leaves on maples
Dotting the hills
And splendor beginning
On hill after hill.

3. *Through the Catskills*

Now the blazing beauty of fall
When Beauty covers mountains
As fall leaves change;
Driving south and east
From 81 to seventeen
To and through the Catskills
We saw mountain after mountain
With only patches of green
Blended with orange, red and yellow.
With the leaves near peak.
As Hopkins would say
The mountains are charged
With the Beauty of God.

4. *Chittenango Falls*

Beyond the blazing beauty of autumn
Comfortable late season colors
Cover the valley surrounding
The dramatic cascade of
Chittenango Falls.

Grandchildren after crossing
The bridge below the Falls
And climbing the other side
Jump through a pile of leaves.
Blazing beauty remains
On hills above the falls
And in spots along the road.

5. Plus One—Thanking God for Beauty

Praise to You my gracious Lord
For red and orange and yellow leaves
For color spread on mountain tops.
Praise to You my gracious Lord
For morning rose across the sky
For daylight bursting through the trees.
Praise to You my gracious Lord
For sunsets spread across the sky
For purple, red and green and gold
Praise to You my gracious Lord
For art and music and the song of birds
Praise to You my gracious Lord
For wildness in the stars
And here on earth,
For mathematical elegance, precise and brief.
Praise to You my gracious Lord
For minds that see Your beauty everywhere,
For awe and wonder at Your works
For Love and Beauty Everlasting.

Cities and Places

Sounds in the Kentucky Hills

At Fort Knox the guns are firing again,
Tank guns on the firing range.
One shot skillfully placed
Can destroy an enemy tank
As demonstrated on television in Iraq.

At the Trappist monastery
The bells are ringing again
Hour by hour calling the monks to prayer.
During meditation one thought
Can penetrate the heavens
Finding the presence of God.

Amid the Kentucky hills
I sit in the Trappist garden
Listening to the bells.
Hearing the boom of the guns
Over the hills.

Year after year
From 1954 to 2004
Since Merton wrote
Complaining of the guns
The guns fire and the bells ring
War and peace in lingering confrontation.

Ottawa

From the west the wind
Blew across Canada
And fluttered the flag
On the Peace Tower,
The heart of Canada's Parliament.
On the cliffs
Above the wild river
The Parliament rose
Over the city.
Bright the sun shone
Over fair flowers
And great art
As Canada's capital
Rejoiced in summer.

The American Embassy
Guarded with concrete,
Fortified and
Looking fortified,
Turret or
Nuclear power plant
Rising in the center
Stood by
The flowering gardens
Edging
Canada's Parliament.

Windblown Canada
Multitongued,
Alive, growing
And free

Snow drapped
In winter,
Flowering
In summer
Refreshes
As contrast
To Fortress
America.
Oh Canada.
Oh, America…

New York

The city is the city, is the city
Of New York.
It has tall, tall buildings
The way a city ought.
It has downtown shows
And dirty politicians.
It has everything a city
Ought to have.

Big ocean liners come
Into its ports.
They take on cargoes
Of tractors and bolts.
They unload loads
Of south grown bananas
Which the stevedores steal
As they lay on the docks.
The city is the city is the city
Of New York.
It has everything a city
Ought to have.

Little helicopters carry you
On
From your downtown throne
To your home and pool
While the poor of the city sit
And sweat in the slums
The city is the city is the city
Of New York
It has everything a city
Ought to have.

San Francisco

As dawn arose over
San Francisco bay
I heard a cable car
Clacking below
My hotel window
Clanging its bell
As it rolled
On the tracks.

Out beyond the bay
Across the wide Pacific
The tsunami victims
Lay on the beach.

The evening before
I passed urban victims
Lying asleep
In the doorways,
Beauty and trauma
As bodies lie scattered
On scenes spectacular
And lovely.

In New York Harbor

There are laughing gulls
At the Statue of Liberty.
I wonder what
They are laughing at,
Laughing with joy,
Rejoicing in liberty,
Or laughing at
Our foolish ventures
Beyond the river's mouth,

Or simply nature
Enjoying the cool
Strong harbor breeze
Blowing off the ocean.

From Summer to Fall

A Response

Cousin Columba,
Servant of God,
Prince of the North
From your Isle of Iona
Send help to your kindred
As we wander the earth.

Help us be servants
To heal and renew
To follow the Lord
As He comforts the poor.

Help us be prophets
To sing out the Word
Confronting the evil
Proclaiming the good.

Help us be writers,
Poets of love
Finding God's wisdom
To shine in the dark.

Ascension Thursday

On Ascension Day
In early May
The sun climbs
The eastern sky
With splendid speed.

At six thirty
When I awake
It's already high
And glaring down
At my waking eye.

Just so the Lord
Arose from a quiet hill
After saying
His last farewell
And like a waking
Bird my soul
Should follow Him.

A Small Operation

Today, a small operation
A participation though slight
In the suffering of Christ
Even so I find You there.

This day You sent me
Your love to sustain me
Your work to distract me
Your presence beside me
My wife to assist me
Your strength to maintain me

Thank You my Friend
For friendship this day.

Now, the Fall

A tiny turtle
Sitting on a log
Its neck stretched
Towards the sun.
I saw it
While walking
The Erie Canal.

Further on I heard
The geese honking.
Now it's early fall
Most of the birds
Are gone,
The swallows,
The redwings,
But geese
And ducks are here
I hear the ducks
Now quacking in the reeds.

The summer is just gone,
A hard summer
Hot with hurricanes
And arthritis.
The fall, the early fall
With just a touch
Of Blazing Beauty
And walks on
The Erie Canal
Is very welcome
Now.

Fall Color

I see robins
And goldenwinged flickers,
Migrating flocks
Searching the grass together.
When I drive the car
On the road over the hill
The birds fly with
Golden wings
Flashing in the sun.
Down the hill a few
Trees now fully changed
To a lighter red and pink
Dotted with green.
Absorbed in beauty
I gaze at the tree,
Remembering the golden wings.
I stop and plunge
Into the beauty,
The overwhelming experience
Of color on top of the hill.

A Fall Reunion

From west to east
From central New York
Down the Thruway
On to the Massachusetts' Pike
The woods were spotted
With spectacular trees.

From east to west
Returning now
After a weekend reunion
With friends from ages past
The woods were changed
Ablaze with color

Friends I've known
Near fifty years
Were mellowed and strong
And like the trees
Were changed with the weather

Returning on this pilgrimage
Somewhat like a time machine
I found echoes of long ago
Along the Charles,
In the Law School yard,
St. Paul's and
Most importantly St. Peter's
Where giving thanks
For turning points
And rescue
I found myself
Again, in the presence
Of God.

The Pumpkin Song: Halloween Fun

I'm a jolly little pumpkin
With a jack o'lantern face.
I have two bright eyes
And a big broad grin
And I shine out on Halloween.

When the witches and the goblins
Come to the door
I peek through the window
And I say:
Boo!

On Human Suffering:
A Series of Poems

New Orleans—Two Poems

I walked once to Jackson Square
Through the iron grillwork.
I have rejoiced in jazz
Casually played on street corners
And in a line of pelicans
As they flew and I walked
Along the Mississippi.
I weep for New Orleans
Lying ruined by Katrina.

The poor are trapped
In flooded houses
With no water to drink
Caught between attic and roof
With the water rising.

The elderly and sick
Are floating on mattresses
Unrescued and isolated
I pray and remain shocked
At the plight of the poor.

New Orleans

I have prayed in St. Louis Cathedral
At one end of Jackson Square,
L'Place des Armes,
I have watched pelicans
Flying in line
While listening to jazz.
I have savored the life
Of New Orleans.

Smashed now by Katrina
Gone, a whole city, gone
Beyond contemplation
Beyond thought
Or understanding.

Hot Summer

Looking back, last summer was hot
Too hot to walk without a hat,
Brain melting hot.

The heat stirred the sea
And the Gulf Stream waters
Produced hurricane after hurricane,
Smashing islands, Caribbean islands,
Flooding farmlands
Along the coastline
Of Central America,
Drowning crops and houses
With water and smashing them
With mud, the mudslides
Burying towns and villages,
Smashing cities,
Destroying New Orleans,
Drowning the poor
Without cars
Or even buses
To escape the flood.

The brain numbing heat
Coupled with arthritis
Caught me in my protected town,
Headache after headache
All summer long.
Even now I feel
The pain in my neck.
I too had a small,
Insignificant share

In the disasters
Caused by this hot,
Too hot and long summer.
Trivial though it was,
I too was smashed.

Sharing Humanity

Without suffering
We would not be human.
Now, that is something
I can say
In favor of suffering.

Yet suffering smashes cities,
Leaves millions freezing
Without shelter,
Leaves mothers, brothers,
Grieving for lost children,
Younger siblings.

Because we understand
Our neighbors more deeply
When we have experienced
Suffering,
We grieve with
Sorrowing mothers,
Lost and starving
Children.
Because we know
What it is to grieve,
We grieve with others.
Because we suffer
We are more fully human,
More fully related
To our grieving
Suffering
Fellow humans.

The Experience of Death

I have the experience of death.
I cried all during the trip
On 81 to 17 and into New Jersey
On the way to my father's funeral.

I kissed her forehead
Cold as clay just after
My mother died,
As in my head I saw
A vision of her flaming ascent
Into heaven, burning
With love for God.

When my mother-in-law,
The week she died
Lay breathing heavily
Mouth wide open,
Struggling for breath,
I watched with her
Each night that week.
I have experienced
And witnessed death,
And death is mighty
And dreadful.

The Lord

"Get behind me, Satan,"
The Lord said to Peter,
And marched towards Jerusalem,
Embracing suffering,
Embracing death
Sharing our experience.

In Matthew, the Lord,
At the end of the ages
Identified with the least
Of us, His brethren.
What you do to them.
You do to Me.

Drinking the cup of life
To the end, to the dregs,
The Lord identifies with us.
Becomes fully one of us,
Grasping suffering,
Challenging oppression
In the worst of its forms,
Sharing our experience,
Through suffering
Becoming fully human,
Becoming more fully related
To His grieving, suffering
Brothers and sisters.

Awesome and wonderful,
Beyond understanding,
The understanding

Of the Lord,
A God Who loves,
Who shares, understands,
Identifies,
This is a God
To love.

Praise to Our Suffering God

Praise to You, my gracious Lord
For sharing in our human lot,
Enduring suffering, embracing death.
Praise to You, my gracious Lord
For carrying the cross, our cross,
Making it Yours, carrying it with us
Praise to You, my gracious Lord
For becoming fully human
Joined to our experience, even unto death.
Praise to You, my gracious Lord
For choosing to create, a growing, evolving, imperfect world,
For choosing to share the suffering of our world.
Praise to You, my gracious Lord
For choosing in the face of inevitable imperfection
To create and save our suffering world.
Praise to You, my gracious Lord
For transforming tragedy and futility
By embracing our experience and making it Yours.
Praise to You, my gracious Lord
For making Love the heart of things.

Transforming Winter

A Late Fall Walk

There's ice on the Erie Canal.
Walking the towpath
On this splendid
Spring-like day
After a snowy
Thanksgiving weekend
I saw some ducks
Testing the edges
Of floating ice.

Snow on the weekend
Decorated the pine trees
Across the street
From my picture window
Offering a winter scene,
Now gone.

Pine trees with snow
Seem dressed for Christmas,
A Thanksgiving weekend
Anticipating the beauty of winter.

As Winter Approaches

Oh that You would rend the heavens
We pray as advent begins
Amidst our suffering war-torn world,
Torn by hurricanes destroying cities
By earthquakes and genocide
Leaving millions, homeless refugees,
Wandering the landscape
As winter approaches
In our advent world.

As winter approaches
Christmas is near.
As winter approaches
Elderly friends
Encountering traumas
Forecast the path
We travel too.
From time to time
You make clear
That Christmas is near.

Natural Law

The Greeks invented
The notion of natural law.
The Romans exploited it
To govern their empire.

God promised to plant
His law in our hearts
Reuniting brother to brother,
Brother to sister,
Parents to children,
Neighbor to neighbor,
Neighbor to alien,
Good Samaritan to wayfarer.
And as the world turns
We find ourselves
Recognizing our brothers
Everywhere as human
As worthy of respect.

One theory follows another
One theory pursues another
Down the ages.
Theories of natural law
Are not natural law.
The breath of God
Moving our hearts
From day to day
With or without theory.
That is natural law.
That law is at work
In America today

Changing racism,
Sponsoring peace
Feeding the poor.

In our Ivory Towers
We build our theories,
Questioning or advocating
The theories of old.
Out in the street
The breath of God
Is feeding the poor,
Transforming our visions,
Freeing prisoners.
From time to time
A glimmer of this
Finds its way
Into out theories.

A Snow-Covered Landscape

As evening advances
The snow-covered houses,
Lawns and pine trees
Are silhouetted against
The grey of the darkening sky.

As night approaches
The grey turns darker
The white though turning
Grey seems still to be white.

The scene altogether
Appears like a classic
Country winter or
Christmas painting,

As seen nevertheless
In my suburban home
Through my large
Plate glass, picture window.

And now, in the time
It took to write this poem
All is dark and
Turned to black.
The bare branches
Of the tree
Stretch out like tangled fingers
Across the night sky
Blacker than that
Grey black sky.

Celtic Music

(For my brother Bill, written
after a telephone conversation)

The keening of the pipes
Can be heard behind
The fiddler's jig,
Can be heard behind
The singing in the pub
And in the Celtic chant.

Celtic music
Wherever it is found
Has a note of sorrow
And longing,
Longing for a world
Gone by
Or yearning for
A world to come,
A world of joy
And beauty beyond sight.

Sorrow and longing,
Eternal striving,
Disappointment and anger
But never despair,
Defiance and challenge
Joy in the face
Of loss and disaster,
The eternal challenge
To the troubles
Of the world.

Celtic music everywhere
In pub, in church,
In concert hall,
Grasping at beauty
At eternal joy
Challenges disaster
And strives ever
For greatness, love
And wonder
And seizes it now
Despite the wreck and ruin.

Winter Comes

Irish tenors appear
At the Landmark Theatre,
Christmas caroling
And singing Danny Boy.
The Lion, the Witch
And the Wardrobe plus
Harry Potter await
In the movies.
On the road to the theatre
Snowflakes fill the air.
Winter is here
With its beauty
And trauma.

The crescent moon
Floats upside down
Early
In the evening sky.
The evening star
Adjacent to the moon
Appears to pull
A rounded sleigh.
Santa Claus
Is reconnoitering
The Christmas trail.
Somewhere from the distant past
Three kings
Are watching
The evening sky.

December Is Mary's Month

May, as Hopkins says,
Is Mary's month
And traditionally
We celebrate
With flowers, processions
And May crownings.

Yet December with
Its cold and snow
Is full of Mary's feasts
As we and she get ready
For the feast of Christmas
Remembering her pregnancy,
Her visit to Elizabeth,
Her joyous song of triumph,
"All generations now
Shall call me blessed."
He has raised the lowly
And thrust the mighty
From their thrones.
In December God remembers
The poor and desperate
Shining in the winter snow
While creating warmth and light
Amid the dark and cold,
And the light shines
In the darkness
And the dark has not
Overcome it.

Our world is glorious
And desperate,
An imperfect creation
For only God is perfect.
To create and love another
Means to make and embrace
A growing, developing, evolving
But imperfect other.

In December, we celebrate
That embrace amidst the dark and cold
And Mary's song of triumph
Rings in the festive dance.

The Days of Christmas

On that first day of Christmas
You sent us Lord
A baby in a cattle trough
Wrapped in swaddling clothes.

On the Feast of Stephen,
The second day of Christmas
You sent us Lord
A prophet martyred
While proclaiming Your glory
While beholding Your opening
Of the heavens.

On the Feast of John,
The third day of Christmas
You sent us Lord
Your friend, the Evangelist John,
Seeing and singing
Good news with amazing insight
Finding the depths of Your presence
In our world.

On all the days of Christmas
You show Your presence
With us in suffering,
Sorrow and joy.

Our Christmas mass,
Our Christmas tree,
The crèche on the mantle
Proclaim your presence.

In the triumph and hardships
Of this imperfect world
Your embrace of this world
Is the source of our joy.

Christmas Girl

A Christmas girl is all my love
A Christmas girl is my delight.
When holly draped the halls of old
And merry Christmas carols rose
Then Greensleeves was often sung
As lovers danced at crowded balls.

When Christmas trees are chopped and trimmed
And lights are sparkling
Through the green and
Presents gather round the tree
Then my Christmas girl begins to glow
And Mary Ann is all my love
And Mary Ann is my delight
And who but pretty Mary Ann.

For Robert Southwell, S.J.

When Greensleeves was
All the rage
A wandering poet sang
What Child is This
To the tune he loved
And preached the wonders
Of Christmas.
Across the hills
In cottages and mansions,
While secretly the children
Sang their catechism
Rejoicing in the days
Of Christmas
Ending on the twelfth night,
The feast of kings
When Jesus sent twelve
Drummers drumming
Out the creed
And drumming still
The poet sang "the Burning Babe"
And followed Him
On to death,
Such our ancestors
In the faith.

VOLUME II
THE JIGSAW PIECE

Jail Break—Four Poems

Instrument of Oppression

We tore the old jail down,
My friends and I.
My efforts were small.
My friend Cathleen
In a cage she built
Fasted for ten days
In front of the jail.

They built a new one
And if a jail is good
This one is good.
Before in the old jail
People behind the bars
Regularly fought the guards
Who responded in kind.

Now they walk
The open floors
And join me in
The conference room
And exit to get
An extra chair
Or to find a paper
And return without a guard
To chat across a table.
The guards are friendly
And easily talk
With their charges.

The rebuilt new jail
Is better by far.
Nevertheless a jail
Is still a jail
And we would fail
If we tried
To tear it down again.

The Symphony

On the way to the symphony tonight
I passed the county jail
Rising high in the center city
Across the street from the Civic Center.
I was in there the other day
Following my list from name to name.

At the symphony we heard
The marvelous music of Verdi's requiem,
A requiem that could be sung
For the prisoners I saw the other day,
A desperate woman pregnant,
Withdrawing from crack cocaine,
A young man lost in youthful troubles
Beyond the usual and his capacity.

What a mess we make of life
And then we bury it, hide it
Behind a facade, smooth walls
Concealing the desperate plight
While we attend the symphony
Just across the street
From the County jail.

Down

Over the wall the young man went
Sliding down a garden hose
From the basketball court
On the roof of the jail,
The old jail, the one we tore down.

Down he went and away.
After three short days
In freedom he called me.
I met him at the church,
The Cathedral, open to all.

My wife and I then walked
With him into court
Where forty deputies
Fully armed awaited him.
I am glad we tore the old jail
    Down.

Imprisoning the Mind

Do not build a prison
For your mind.
Discipline yes,
Prison no.
Let your thoughts
Go freely abroad.

Mathematics, science, logic
Have a disciplined
Cutting edge that
Let's us see
What otherwise
We could not find.

But to insist
That only mathematical
Thought can find the truth
Is to construct
Strong prison bars
Across your mind.

Melting the Snow

February Robins

February fifteenth
I hear some robins
Clucking in a nearby tree.
The snow is melting.
Today the temperature
Will rise to forty.

At breakfast my wife
Asked whether I had seen
The snowdrops, early flowers
Peeking through the snow
In front of our house.
And there they were,
Clustered together,
Snow white blooms
Unopened, emerging
On top of green stems.

Each year I see robins
Before St. Patrick's day.
To find the robins
Is a game to celebrate spring.
In my game, however,
February robins do not count.

Arthur Phillips

Symbiosis is the word
Which Arthur,
Dr. Arthur Phillips,
Professor of Biology,
Expert in plant
Microbiology,
Took from his subject
To understand,
To celebrate,
To apply
To family, friends
And nursing home,
One plant, one person
Intertwining,
Supporting another,
Mutual support,
The friendship of all,
Symbiosis extended
Across the world
Describing God's work,
The spirit of creation.

Arthur died this week.
I brought him communion
On Monday,
A few days before
He left to join
In symbiosis
With the saints
In heaven.
We closed our prayers

By saying the Pater Noster
In Latin, a scholar
To the end.

I knew Arthur
Late in his life
For two years or three,
A gentle man,
Polite and kindly
Considerate of all,
A genius who discussed
Science, evolution,
Plate tectonics,
Philosophy,
Even law.
What have you written
He asked, and then
Ordered my book
And read it
At least in part.

A New Englander,
Descended from Puritans
And Irish and Welsh,
Devoted to Notre Dame
Where he learned
Philosophy and science,
He remembered Cambridge
Where he took
His Ph.D. at M.I.T.
With friendly affection.
We shared memories
Of life along the Charles.

Gentleman, Christian,
Scientist, scholar,
A gentle, kindly man,
An inquiring mind,
Who would gladly
Be taught
And gladly teach.
I shall miss him,
Our Monday talks and
The symbiosis
Of the thoughts we shared.

Creating and Denying Knowledge

Science, Biology, Physics,
The genome, DNA,
Subatomic particles,
The Heisenberg uncertainty
Principle, amazing
What disciplined probing
Can discover
Plodding carefully
Over, time,
Accumulating knowledge.

Science as a discipline
Wielding method,
Scientific method,
Hypothesizing, verifying,
Rather endeavoring
To falsify,
Checking out
Always careful
Inspired at times
Diligently inquires,
By its method
Produces marvels.

With its cutting edge,
Probing and checking
The discipline of science
Let's us see,
Let's us know,
Let's us understand
What otherwise

Without science
We would ignore
Pass over,
Muddle.

Imperial science
On the other band
Dominating, controlling
Vetoing other knowledge,
Not sufficiently mathematical,
Acquired with methods
Unknown to science,
Perchance through common sense
Or human recognition
Of suffering, virtue
Or struggle, that scientism
Draws the shades
Around the laboratory
Shutting out the world,
Rejecting knowledge
And human understanding.

New Snow

A snowy weekend
In late February
Began with an inch or two
Of snow on Friday morning.

On Friday afternoon
The sun through the trees
Made patterns of light
And shadow on the snow.

The Downy woodpecker
Black and white
With a bright red spot
Pecked at the suet feeder.
A nuthatch followed
Hanging upside down
To get at the white chunk
Of pseudo meat.
The sun shone pleasantly
On the new fallen snow.

Late February Snow

I just took a walk
Over plowed roads
Through the February snow
While light flakes floated
Around my head.
I see the falling snow
Now through my picture window
Drifting thickly but gently
Between me and the pine trees.
A goldfinch in its winter coat
Is pecking at the feeder.
The late February snow
Has covered the snowdrops
And chased the February robins
Back to the Pompey woods
Where they winter instead of
Flying south to escape the cold.
In a week or two they will return
And snowdrops will emerge
In early March
The way they should
And spring will mix
With winter
In the proper order
Of life in Onondaga County.

A Winter Sunrise

On a wintry morning
Across the snow covered roofs
Across the smoking chimneys
Across the pine trees
Above the eastern hills
Amidst pink and purple clouds
I saw the sun rise bright and golden.

Woodpeckers

After the robins
And the red winged blackbirds
Due in two weeks or three
I then will look for flickers,
Goldenwinged flickers,
Pecking on the ground
Flashing golden wings,
A family, I discovered,
Quite different than
The Downy woodpecker
Who pecks at my suet feeder
In the winter snow,
And quite different again
Than the pileated magnificent one
Who clattered through my campsite
One summer long ago.

Flickers, I have seen
Across our country
Amid cactus plants
Tall and prickly
Pecking their holes
Near the top of
The tall green shaft.
The Arizona flicker
Is a different species
But interbreeds with
Our local Northern flicker,
Random mutation,
Evolution by separation
And different breeding groups.

Yet woodpeckers all
Stand straight up propped
And steadied by strong tail
Against the tree with
Straight and sharp bill
Poised to strike, to probe
To peck and have
Bright spots here and there,
Plainly related, evolved
By random mutation
Again in different breeding groups.

All this the bird book
Tells me based on taxonomy
But not yet on DNA.
Nevertheless the book
Is probably right
And will predict
What DNA will find.

The human mind has a remarkable ability
To see and discern
Patterns in woodpeckers,
Nature, language,
Life and fellow human beings.

Breaking Patterns

Something there is
That doesn't love
A pattern,
That wants to see
It differently
To reshape and
Shake up
To redesign.

Try measuring
The speed of an electron
While predicting its location,
So much for iron clad rules
That govern the universe.
Consider random mutation
And the vast proliferation
Of changing patterns
Among plants and animals.

In human thought
The development
Of alternate patterns
As thought leads to thought
Leaping from construct to construct
Is called "creativity".
In biology the proliferation
Of species as genes
Mutate and survive
Is considered the product of chance
And physicists confronted
With uncertainty develop

Chaos theory to cope
With incoherence.

What a shame and
What a bore to live
From age to age
In a civilization that
Exactly resembles
The ways of our ancestors.
The Eternal Shape Changer
Has provided us
With chance and mutation
With development and change
With opportunity to grow
And reform.
"Repent", He says, and believe
The Good News, change
Your lives, develop and grow.

Early Spring

The rain is sweeping away
The snow pack
Melted by the rising temperature.
The rain is the cutting edge
Of returning spring
Almost a week early
This year.

Oh, we will have more snow,
Spring snow I call it,
Snow that falls
After the first robin.
Ordinarily we have
Eighteen inches of March snow
And six inches in April.
At the moment we are
Six inches short
Of average snowfall
With our slim hundred
And thirteen inches.

But as the weather warms
And between the snow flakes
I am ready to search
For a March robin.
I have a week
Until St. Patrick's Day.

For St. Patrick's Day

Cathleen

Suppose the Countess Cathleen,
Cathleen ni Hoolihan
Immigrated to the United States
Or came for a visit.
What riots would she stir then?
Or revolutions prompt?

Or would she be stuffy,
Middleaged and conservative
As if to preserve the old ways
In a foreign land?
Did she stand behind
The Bishop, Dagger John,
When he threatened to burn the city
When the next convent was ignited
Or when he opposed
The free wheeling thought
Of Orestes Brownson
And insulted him to his face?

Singing "I'm a poor stranger
And far from my own",
Would she feed the poor
And defend the oppressed?
I thought I saw her
In the cage my friend Cathleen
Had built in front
Of the jail.

Does she wander through
The soup kitchens,
The food pantries, aiding
The helping hands
To the immigrant,
Beguiling many a young lad
Or inspiring girls with bright eyes?

Now that Ireland's free
Does she reign again
Or retire to the shadows
Hanging on the walls,
An honored portrait
From the past?
Or does she wander
Free, across the world
Wherever Irish go

Knowing their past,
Revolution and oppression,
The bitterness of famine,
The deeds of great warriors,
The songs of poets,
Sung by the wayside
Or in the legendary
Halls of kings?

Again I think I see her
Wandering through the cities
Wherever good deeds are done
Or high songs are sung,
The searching spirit
Of the Celt
Striving not for glory
But for eternal beauty.

Purple Crocuses and Spring Birds

Spring came in with
A rush, a week ago,
Warm weather, bright sunshine,
Robins, grackles, redwings
All at once
Canadian geese honking overhead,
Buzzards floating here and there,
And killdeer, a migrating flock.
I thought I heard their call
And went exploring
And there they were
Running all around the grass.

Spring was a week early
And now we have spring snow
Not more than two inches
On the ground with purple crocuses poking
Their blooms through
The white fluff.

Today again I saw
A flock of robins, and
Heard the chuck, chuck
Of grackles flying.

Nevertheless it will be
A cold St. Patrick's day tomorrow and
A cold day for a parade
On Saturday. I think
We may watch the parade
On television and listen

To Irish songs on disc,
Watching the grackles and
The purple crocuses
Through my picture window,
My spectacular view
Of winter, spring and fall.

The Canal: An Early Spring Walk

One goose watches
While the other eats.
I saw them at the end
Of the trail on the Erie Canal.
Otherwise there were grackles
Only grackles and
A gull or two
As I took an early
Spring walk along the canal.

The grackles flew,
Chucking, back and forth
Across the canal
In the bright sunshine
Of a 70 degree
Early Spring day,
One of the first
And during my first
Spring walk along
The snow cleared towpath.

I know that in
A month or two
There will be orioles
Flying with golden orange
Flashes across the canal
Where now there are
Only grackles announcing
Spring.

Purple Crocuses and Bees

On returning from a walk
I found the purple crocuses,
A flock of purple crocuses,
Fully open in front
Of my old maple tree.
The bees were busily
Gathering nectar
From the purple crocuses
On this first warm day
In early spring.

Lenten Reflections

Lenten Reading

The Hebrew prophets
Isaiah through Habakkuk
Make good Lenten reading
With a sprinkle
Of Winston Churchill
And Franklin Roosevelt
During the early days
Of the Second World War

The prophets were amazed
And rejoiced at the fall.
Of Babylon, that terrifying city,
And the Persian Conqueror,
King Cyrus, who ordered
Their return to Judea
And the rebuilding
Of the Temple
In Jerusalem.

Churchill standing alone
When the French surrendered
And his troops fled
Across the Channel
While holding Hitler
For a moment at Dunkirk,
Said one evening over drinks,
I know how I can win
This war and he did.

From disaster to disaster
The world triumphantly advances
As the Redeemer's Crucifixion
Began a movement.
Which converted the Roman
Empire in three hundred years,
And continues with advances
And declines ever forward
Until today and beyond,

Because the Holy Ghost
Over the bent world broods
We know we shall see
Orioles flashing golden orange
Where now the snow is melting
And only grackles fly.

Christ and the Poor

When you love the poor
You love me,
That is an essential
Message of the Christ
Reinforced powerfully
By His becoming
The poor and suffering one.

Have pity on me,
The strong and mighty
God calls out, and
Pity all my poor,
Little and suffering ones.
What you do to these,
The least of my brethren
You do unto Me.

You were not present
When Veronica wiped My Face
But you can wipe
The face of the poor.
You were not there
When I was thirsty
But you can dig
A well in Africa
Slacking the thirst
Of my sisters and brothers
Far from running water.

You were not there
When I was beatened
By Roman soldiers
But you can visit
Me in prison
Where my sisters and brothers
Are hidden from sight
Behind tall white walls
Concealing their sufferings

The Sacrifice of Christ

A willing heart
Is the sacrifice
You wish O God,
The prophet prayed
And said:
"Here I am,
I come to do
Your will."

The sacrifice of Christ
Is not a blood offering
To satisfy the wrath
Of an angry God,
Rather it is God
Accepting the limitations,
The sufferings, the disasters
Of humankind.

Rather it is God
Challenging the powers
Of the Earth and Empire.
Do your worst, He says,
Tear this Temple down,
In three days
It will be whole again
Stirring life
Throughout your Empire.

Do your worst, He says,
But in your streets
And forums

And across your
Roman roads
Love will spread
Brother will turn
To brother,
Sister to sister
Sons to father and mother.

I will be first
Leading My people
Challenging your might
Reestablishing love.
Here I am Lord
I come to do
Your will.
As I cleanse
The earth and lead
My people
In Your love,
A willing heart
Is the sacrifice
Offered to the Father
By the Son.

Towards Easter

Advancing Spring

Twilight at eight o'clock,
It was a cool
Early April day
But I saw ducks
In a flooded meadow,
A phoebe flycatcher
Fliting there in the brown grass
From stalk to stalk,
My first this spring.
A mocking bird flashing
White wing bars
Invading my yard
And killdeers not now
In flocks but couples
And spring advances
As the sunlight lingers.

Recognition

Recognition is not
A scientific term.
Although scientists
Experience that
Brilliant flash
Of insight when
Data coalesces
In a pattern.

Archimedes once
Ran naked in the street
Shouting "Eureka",
Rejoicing at his insight
And a theory
Can be described
As a connected
Series of insights.

Recognition is
An insight into
Persons or relations,
The moment when
One says, my wife
Is good, not
Beautiful but good
Although she may
Be beautiful too.

To recognize the goodness,
The honesty, the sincerity,
The moral struggle

Or suffering of another
Is a moment of insight
Which I call
Recognition, the discovery
That another is human.

Recognition is
A high moment
In human relations,
A moment when love,
Deep love becomes
Possible, when
Life among friends
Suddenly seems
Profoundly worthwhile.

Recognition is not
A scientific term
But scientists
Experience recognition.
Without that
Vital moment

They may not be
Fully human,
Relating to fellow
Human beings
In friendship and
In love.

Recognition and Verification

Recognition cannot
Be verified.
But it can be
Checked out,
Examined for fit
With the rest
Of our knowledge
With our experience
Of this human being.

Does this piece
Of red confetti
Or this piece
Of a jigsaw
Puzzle fit
The pattern
We are forming
Or perceiving?
Will future
Insights coalesce
With this
Exciting moment?

Verification or
The scientific
Process of falsification
Has an important
Place in scientific
Method and is
An important mode
Of checking out.

But in the range
Of human skills
Verification is but
One mode of checking out.
Other modes are necessary
To survival and
To puzzle out
The patterns in
The world around us.

In law, in love,
In military operations
Verification is neither
Necessary nor possible
And we would not
Survive if verification
Dominated our methodology.

Focal Points

When the day at
Montezuma Swamp
Advances towards
Evening and
The geese in flights
Of hundreds or thousands
Crowd the sky
Descending to the water,

The snow geese often
Are hard to find
Amid the migrating tribes.
But when the telescope
Focuses and we see
White, snow white geese
Whose wings are tipped
With black, spectacular
In flight or swimming
In flocks out, far out
Towards the middle
Of the open lake,
That vision remains
And returns far past spring migration.

My brother Bill once offered
An image of white confetti floating in the air
Surrounding one piece
Of red confetti
Which became the focal
Point of what he called
The Confetti Generation.

Just so amid
The whirl of human events
The clash of theories,
The political struggle,
The culture wars,
The Easter Triduium,
Passover, Good Friday
And the Resurrection
Repeatedly focus
Our attention on
God's presence
In our world.

Springtime

Blossom Time

Great numbers of yellow dandelions
Now dot the fresh unmown lawns
Like stars on a clear night
Shining in a green sky.

The world is blossom lovely.
Flowering crabs (some of them
Will produce edible fruit),
Magnolias and green
Blossomed maples beautify
The landscape in Dewitt.

Even at Town Hall
Near Ryder Park
Hundreds of dandelions
Brighten the lawns.
I am proud of the
Town of Dewitt.

At Beltane in the beginning of May,
The blossom time of spring,
When tulips wave in cool/warm breezes
Dewitt is transformed
Into the Land of Oz.
Beauty then is found
In yard after yard.

Mary Ann and our grandchildren
Planted the 170 tulips in our front yard
And others bred and
Diversified the ancestral
Tulip, showing that
Human persons loved
And labored for beauty,
And that we are co-creators.
But the fundamental
Underlying beauty of the spring
Reveals a Person who shares,
Communicates and appreciates.
Beauty everywhere is
A form of shared experience.

Ideas and Subatomic Particles

Subatomic particles
Appear to be
The most basic
Building blocks of matter
In our universe of
Billions of galaxies and stars
Together with the forces,
The strong force, the weak
Force etc. which
Bind them together.

All else are ways
Of organizing subatomic particles
Including atoms,
Molecules, chemical
Mixtures, DNA and
RNA, the marvelous
Arrangements of life,
The genome, the pills
I take, the shoes,
I wear, the paper
I am writing on.
These arrangements of
Subatomic particles
Essentially are ideas,
That is ways of arranging things and
Making them work.
Some ideas, this paper
For example are
Human constructions.

Others appear to float.
Around in the universe
Gathering and building
One upon another
To create the marvels
We find as we gaze
Out and explore.

Oh, sometimes the
Subatomic particles
And the atoms
They gather into
Require rearranging
And that often
Takes force, mighty
Force to tear apart
An atom and rearrange
Its subatomic particles.
The sun emitting heat and light
Torn from its atoms
In a nuclear furnace
Is constant rearrangement
Within an idea.

The supernovas exploding
Rearranged the helium
And hydrogen atoms of
The early universe to
Create more complex
Arrangements of subatomic
Particles into all
The elements now set
In orderly pattern in
The periodic table
And used in further

Structures, for example,
The carbon building blocks
Of life, further structures
Which essentially are ideas,
Patterns, themselves
Arranged in further
Patterns described
By scientific laws.
I wonder where all
The patterns, the scientific
Laws, the ideas that
Arrange the universe,
I wonder where
They came from.

Green Pastures and Cool Waters

Mid May

Mid May, an overcast day,
Walking on the towpath
I saw yellow warblers
In the bushes and trees
Along the Erie Canal
And I heard an oriole
Singing his bubbling song.
One day I shall see
The oriole fly
Flashing golden orange
Touched with black.

Providence

A deterministic universe
Such as that imagined
By Laplace, early in
The nineteenth century
Would exclude
A providential God
Who intervenes
From time to time
Out of love
For his creatures.

The Heisenberg uncertainty
Principle and Darwin's
Theory of Evolution
With its random mutation
And survival of the fittest
Put an end to total
Determinism as a
Scientific Theory.

But chance as a factor
In a developing universe
Not only provides flexibility
And a way for species
To survive the clash
Of gigantic systems
Like plate tectonics
And the changing climate
Plus a stray asteroid or two,

Chance also leaves gaps
In deterministic scientific laws,
The uncertainty principle
Allows for statistical regularities
But not absolute predictions,
Allows for providential alteration
And free will for thinking humans.

An apparent random mutation
Inspired from above
Could mold a developing species.
An inspiration freely
Accepted by a searching
Person could change
A career and a destiny.
Subtly by modest intervention,
Gently without bruising further
A broken reed
God can shepard His people
Leading them to
Green pastures and cool waters.

The First Heron

A great blue heron
Flew above and down
My street today
Just above the treetops
Enormous wings
Flapping slowly,
The first this spring.

The bird flew above
Trees with new
Green leaves and
Trees with blossoms
Across fields of
Dandelions and tulips.
My street is
Blossom wonderful

And goldfinches
Yellow and black
Eat thistle seeds
At my feeder and
A great blue heron
Slowly flies
Above it all.

Spring Is Advancing

The song sparrow sings
From the top of the tree
Down in the garden
The robin hops along
Tulips are dancing
All around the tree
Spring is advancing
On the southern breeze

A Rational Universe

Visiting the Jail

A year ago
He sold me
A black suit,
A pleasant, talkative
Energetic salesman
We had a friendly
Exchange which sticks
In my memory.

His face and neck
Had knife wounds when
I met him in jail
In the hospital pod
Sitting on a bed
Wounded and weak.

He had retired.
His wife divorced him.
His girlfriend knifed him
And she in turn was
In critical care
Leading to his arrest.

Lilac Time

Late in May
Is lilac time
In the Onondaga
Countryside, deep
Vibrant color in
Farmyard after farmyard.

I went out exploring
Down the Apulia road
Past Jamesville beach
Through high hills and
Fertile valleys to
Apulia and Apulia
Station and then I
Saw a back road
Through the hills
And discovered
An isolated lake in Lebanon Hollow,
A nature preserve
Virtually wild
With a boardwalk
Through the wet lands
Built by volunteers.

I heard a frog croak
Sounding like a twang
From a cello string
Pulled once and vibrating.
I saw a redwing
On a branch stretching
Over an inlet

Monarch of his pond.
Near the water was
A kingbird, white
Tail rim flashing
As he darted after
Flies, and then back
From the lake on
A small twig of
A dead tree almost
Blending with the wood
A humming bird sat,
Sharp little beak
Stretching out like
An extension of the
Branch until I
Moved and it flitted
Away with wings
Vibrating rapidly.

Then still wondering
At nature's marvels
I drove to Fabius
And back to Pompey
Through lilac time
In Onondaga's countryside.

Supporting a Rational Universe

When Greeks rejoiced
In the dawn of
Rationality, philosophers
Rejected the ancient
Brawling, debauching gods
Seeking instead one
Rational God who guaranteed.
The rationality of the universe.

When joined with
Hebrew thought
The West had found
A personal God
A loving Creator
Who visited and cared
For His people
While supporting rational
Thought, good character
And an intellectual
Understanding of
Our universe.

With ups and downs
And struggles with
Barbarian raids
While monks prayed,
Thought and scribbled
Diligently, that vision
Laid the rational
Foundation for modern
Science. Now the

Question is—has
Science destroyed
That vision of a
Rational, caring God
Who supports the structure
Of a universe governed
By his rational, scientific
Laws?

Troublesome

Troublesome, troublesome,
Troublesome to scientists
Intent on excluding God
Is what they call
The anthropic principle.
Here we are, we humans,
An intelligent species
Knowing science and
Tracing scientific laws
Throughout the stars and
Galaxies, gazing at beauty.
If we are here, then
The universe must be
Suitable for our evolution,
The evolution of an
Intelligent species.

And indeed it is.
If gravity were just
A smidgen stronger
The universe would collapse,
The earth would plunge
Into the sun before
Life began to evolve.
In a universe of two
Dimensions we would
Have difficulty eating.

It takes ten billion
Years or more for life
To evolve, for a first

Generation of stars
To convert helium and
Hydrogen into carbon
And
Explode so a third
Generation of the universe
Can use carbon and
Oxygen to evolve
Over 3 billion years
Or more the stages
Leading to intelligent life
And to persons who can trace
And understand the development of stars,
Planets and intelligent
Life. Altogether
It looks like a universe
Intelligently planned.

Roses and Dandelions

There are no roses
In the rose garden
By the university
But the first crop
Of dandelions
Have turned the lawns
Yellow and gone
To seed, all white
Blowing in the wind
And the honeysuckle
Bush is blooming
In my backyard
While cardinals sing
And fly across the lawn.

Spring Walk with Goslings

Families of geese with
Goslings of all sizes,
Mostly small, walk
And swim along
The Erie Canal.
Barnswallows swoop
Low across the water.
Carp are splashing
Almost walking in
The shallow stream.
On a sand bar
Camouflaged and hidden
A sandpiper runs
While grackles and
Catbirds make noise
In the background.
A yellow warbler
Or two and some goldfinch
Make it an altogether
Satisfactory spring walk.

Stephen Hawking

I know you Stephen Hawking,
Physicist extraordinaire,
Analyst for Black Holes.
I recognize your style
And admire your courage,
Brilliance and clarity
Of explanation—and
The games you play
With God. Oh there is
No explanation I can
Find, you say, so
You win, O God,
You must be there, but wait, try this,
A possible explanation.
Sorry God. You lose.

Scientists and creationists
Seem to seek the presence
Of God only where they
Can't explain, where no
Theory has yet developed,
That they say is where
God may be, that is
God's realm. Scientists
Seek to limit that area
While creationists want
To expand the unknown
Field. Both strategies—
The same, God's realm
Is the realm of darkness.

My God lives in the light
Where intellectual brilliance
Shines, where the universe
Sparkles with ideas,
Insights and scientific
Laws. God's intelligence
Shines forth like sparkles
From shook foil
The universe is full
Of beauty and intelligence.

Don't look for God,
Stephen Hawking where
You can't understand.
Find Him instead in
The brilliance of scientific
Theory, in the uniform
Presence in the universe
Of scientific law.

God, After All, Is a Creator

Here we are on
A small planet
Circling our galaxy,
The Milky Way, on
A spiral arm near
Its outer edge
Looking out and back
Towards a billion stars
In just our galaxy,
Looking beyond towards
Billions of galaxies
Rapidly expanding,
As Hubble found.

The universe appears
Rationally arranged
For our intelligent
Life to emerge
And contemplate the
Evolving, expanding universe.
But why would a powerful
Intelligent person with
Great force and brilliance
Create billions of stars
So just our planet
Could harbor intelligent
Searching human persons?

You know He just might.
But probably not and
There is another answer:

Namely lots of planets,
Scattered throughout
Let's say ten per galaxy
Harboring life adventuring
On the way to intelligence.

Why, O God, Do You Regard Man?

What is man, O God,
That you have regard for him
The psalmist cries out.
Today the skeptic gazing at
The vastness of the universe
The billions of stars and galaxies
Challenges the sense of the Biblical
God. Why he asks would
Anyone so powerful as an
Imagined creator of the universe
Trouble to hear the prayers
And rescue the person who
Prays, why would He have
Regard for the smallness
Of man? He then invokes
The virtue of humility and
The dethroning of earth from
Its imagined central place
In ancient cosmology.
Recognizing our smallness,
He says, should lead us
To understand that a God
If He exists would not
Be our God, the God of the Bible
Who is concerned for each
Of His creatures and hears our prayers.

But You, O God, are powerful
And wonderful beyond human
Conception. The skeptic seeks
To limit your powers and love.

While pretending in view of
The vastness of the universe
To enhance that power and
Separation from us, he
Overlooks the true wonder
Of your strength and love
Which can make flowers grow,
Vein violets as Hopkins says,
Join subatomic particles into
Atoms, molecules, crystals,
Mountains, galaxies, while
Creating life and the intricacies
Of the genome and the
Intelligence of the human brain.

You are powerful beyond
Our conceptions, O Lord
And can regard the small
And troubled, not breaking
A bruised reed while raising
Mountains, planets and galaxies.

Your love, O Lord, is the
Greatest of Your wonders.
Your power is immense.
You have regard for Your creature
On planet X in a far galaxy
And hear our prayers here
On earth, a small planet
On a spiral arm of the
Milky Way. The skeptic
In the name of humility
Seeks, O Lord, to diminish
Your power and the wonder
Of Your love.

Crying out to God

In the jail conference
Room, he sat and wept
And cried out to God
For mercy. He was
Worried about his
Children, left fatherless
By a hasty deed in
Difficult circumstances.

As I listened to him
I remembered feeling
Trapped when I was
Young, unable to
Wiggle loose from the
Circumstances of life.
I remember my prayer
In the pews of St. Peter's
Church profoundly in
Awe of the mercy God
Had shown me when
Only he could find
The way for me.
I remembered the many
Times when I cried out
To God on behalf of
My little ones seeking
Rescue and a path for
Them and I remember
The doors He opened
And the way He found.

Were he and I deluded
Along with the many
Others I have heard
Crying out to God
In jail,in prison,
In war and desparate
Circumstances? Each
Morning I pray, "Thank you, God, for constant
Care and protection." And
I know the times and places.
I know when God has
Rescued me.

Co-Creators

Mid June and the roses
Are blooming in the Rose
Garden at Thornden Park.
I passed them on the way
Home from visiting the Jail.

One man I talked to
Had a series of seizures
The guards thought he was
Faking and had no time
For him while he
Stuttered attempting to talk.

The rose garden flourishes
Because, the paper reports,
One hundred and seventy
Volunteers labor regularly
Cultivating, pruning, planting
While we have ten screeners
And twenty visitor advocates
Visiting regularly in the Jail.

We are co-creators with God.
Roses flourish because
Generations of gardeners
Have cultivated and selectively
Bred to produce the vast
Varieties blooming in the garden.

How have we managed to
Produce the variety of

Circumstances in the Jail?
Not entirely in the Criminal
Justice System although
We have labored diligently.
Our County Jail is descended
From Quaker idealism
Practically tried in
Philadelphia in the Walnut
Street Jail and distorted
And changed and developed.
Our present Jail is better
By far than its predecessors.

On the Feast of Corpus Christi

"My God, my God, why
Have you abandoned me,"
The Lord Jesus cries out
From his cross, quoting
The twenty-second psalm.
I have heard the poor
Cry out in desperate tones
Seeking love and rescue.
The Lord Jesus joins
His voice to theirs.
"Deliver my soul from
The sword, my life from
The power of the dog."
Continues the psalm.

And His Father heard
The Lord Jesus and
He rose up recreating
The Temple of God, transforming
Religion, starting a movement
That continues to this day
Allowing the poor to cry out
In desperation and hope
To God and the Lord Jesus,
To recall and understand,
To extend pierced hands,
To suffer with and rescue
Them. And the psalm
Continues to praise God,
"For He has not despised
Or abhored the affliction

Of the afflicted and He
Has not turned his face
From Him but has heard
When He cried out to Him."

Quoting the twenty-second
Psalm, the Lord Jesus
Cried out in hope and
We too can cry out in hope
For the Lord has shared
Our suffering and joined
Us in our evolution and
Co-creation, however stumbling,
Of this world He gave us.

Fourth of July

Systems out of Whack

Fires on the west coast,
Rain, heavy rain on the east,
A hot, too hot summer
Has begun. They're chopping
Ponderosa pine on the rim
Of the Grand Canyon stopping
The forest fire there while
Binghamton is flooded, the
Susquehana and the Delaware
Overflowing, Pennsylvania
Is devastated, Wilkes-Barre
Evacuated. When we put
The systems out of whack
That's what a week of
Heavy rain can do and its
Not yet the Fourth of July.

An Old-Fashioned Fourth

On the Fourth of July
I saw an oriole in the grass
By the side of the road
Where I stopped to rest
And pray awhile on a long
Walk by the side of the lake

We spent the Fourth of July
At the summer cottage where
The bird life has an exotic
Touch. Hummingbirds, for
Example, visit in the evening.
A great blue heron flies
Down the lake each morning
Followed by a flotilla of geese
And then a kayak or two

It was an old fashioned
Traditional Fourth of July
With grandchildren and amateur
Home-style fireworks, a boat
Parade and flares lining the
Lake. We placed our flares
And built a fire and watched
The Roman candles brighten
The sky. Television is virtually
Banished and we suppressed
The news, staying away from
America's real but phony war
And celebrating old fashioned
Patriotism.

The Rocket's Red Glare

While we were celebrating
A quiet Fourth of July
The nations set off rockets
As we discovered on the Fifth
When we turned on television
And tapped into the news.

To celebrate our pride and
Independence we sent a
Spaceship off towards the
Space station, a step on
The way to the moon where
We may one day find water,
A large rocket for the Fourth.

North Korea chose the Fourth
To challenge us by firing
One large rocket which failed
And fell into the sea about
A minute after launch and
Five intermediate range rockets
Which may, another day, reach
Japan thereby destroying
The peace of our world, a
Small rocket, perhaps, to cause
The war which will end all rockets.

Anniversary

We celebrated
Our 30th anniversary
In the jail, last night
Serving ice cream
And cake to the
Prisoners. We had
Drummers and a poet
And we moved from
Pod to pod with
Our party while the
Guards helped out.
We sat at the tables
And talked with the
Prisoners sharing
The Jail Ministry
Story. It could not
Have happened
Twenty years ago.
I'm glad we tore
The old jail down.

August

No Hurricanes Yet

As I sit on my front lawn
Under the shade of my old maple
Tree on this the second hottest
Day of the year (yesterday was
The hottest), while in the
Middle East a serious war
Is going forward and people are
Dying in the bombing, I feel
A breeze and hear the bells of
Our new church for the first
Time, I remember your friendship
O Lord amid our struggles and
Co-creation and note the
Absence of hurricanes this summer
Even though it is early August.

To See the Squirrels Run

Half a dozen little squirrels
Running around my yard
Frolicking in the street, just
Down from the trees across
The road. One little one
Looked up at me unafraid.
But prepared to run. How
Lovely is life in children and
Squirrels when it is young and
They have just begun. As I
Sit under my ancient maple tree
On this the hottest day of the year
With Israel invading Lebanon
I think what fun to see
The squirrels run.

Juncos

The junco is a northern bird,
Rather neat in spring and fall
And sometimes amid the winter
Snow with black hood, grey back
And two white tail feathers which
Flash when it flies. I rejoice
To see them at my feeder in
The fall and spring perhaps
On their way to Canada.

I just discovered them in the
Bushes and trees by our cottage
And saw a mother junco bathing
In a puddle, still there from the
Heavy rain, flapping her wings and
Splashing the water, enjoying the pause
As I enjoy the cottage by the lake.

Cedar Waxwings

In fall and sometimes in winter
Buff colored cedar waxwings
With their tiny crests and spots
Like wax brightly colored on
Wings and tail gather in small
Flocks to eat the berries on
My backyard bushes. I
Look forward to their visits.

At the cottage we have a tree
Rising high near, very near
The water and then another
On our neighbor's plot not
Far away. Several times this
Summer I have seen there small
Groups of cedar waxwings playing
Flycatcher, darting out between
The trees, hovering a moment
To catch a fly and return to a
Tree branch, to watch and dart
Again. It is a busy merry sight

I have seen the same behavior
In Canada by lakesides at
Camping spots. Once a small
Lake had wooden posts at
Intervals all around the pond
Cedar waxwings on each post
Would dart out to play the
Flycatcher game. Also at
Green Lakes higher in the air

Because they were flying from
Higher trees they would dart
Out to the middle of the lake
Hover and return. So spring
And summer, fall and winter
Buff colored cedar waxwings
With their tiny crests and bright
Colored spots brighten the landscape.

Discerning the Presence of God

Recognizing God: Cosmology

Look, look, look
Look up and out and
See the wonders of the
Heavens, thousands of stars,
Our galaxy, the Milky Way
All within our sight.
Look again, look at
The moon, the Big Dipper,
The North Star, gaze at
The Wonder and Glory.
The universe is charged
With the Grandeur of God.

Then read, analyze,
Understand. Billions of
Stars, billions of galaxies
All rushing apart as Hubble
Discovered. Wonder after wonder,
A universe to study with
Newton's geometry and
Einstein's great theory,
Billions of stars, expanding
With greater rapidity, the
Further away they are,
Cosmic radiation witnesses
To the Big Bang, apparently
A moment of creation with

Subatomic particles bubbling
Freely until joined in atoms
By gravity, the strong and
Weak force, etc., Joined
At first in simple atoms,
Helium and hydrogen which
Composed the first stars as
Gravity pulled them together.

But then think. Our atomic
Structures are arranged
Logically in the periodic
Table, a logical structure
Which emerged from three
Generations of stars and
Exploding supernova. Then
Perceive the anthropic
Principle. All is suitably
Arranged for the evolution
Of intelligent life including
The necessary carbon and oxygen
Manufactured by exploding
Supernova, a marvelous
Process well arranged.

Then look back at the
Heavens, wonder and beauty,
Beauty everywhere and
The universe governed throughout
By scientific laws which
Our intelligent species is
Gradually uncovering and
Understanding. Are we
Meant to see beauty and
Discover the order and

Laws, the marvelous
Structure and splendor of
A vast, developing universe?

The world is charged says
Hopkins with the grandeur
Of God, it flames out and
Sparkles with ideas and beauty.
Analysis and logical structures
Are necessary to understanding.
But look, gaze, wonder
And recognize, here is
A Person of vast intelligence
And love of beauty, who
Wants intelligent creatures
To recognize and understand
The marvelous structure and
Enjoy the adventure of discovery
And savor the beauty found
In everything including the
Clear precision of mathematical
Formulas and the dancing delight
Of subatomic particles and quantum
Physics. But yet remember
That recognition is not science
But one person encountering
Another in love and splendor.

The Genetic System

For sixty million years or more
We have lived in the age of
Mammals. Our ancestors once.
Were small nocturnal animals
But after the asteroid struck
Proliferated
Into saber toothed
And Siberian tigers, mammoths,
Elephants, whales, foxes, deer,
Squirrels, chimpanzees and humans.

The random mutation of genes
Supplemented by natural selection
Was the engine that drove this vast
Diversification. While mammals were
Developing into many species, the
Remaining dinosaurs continued in
A similar manner to change into
Birds of great variety and kinds
Aided perhaps by isolated breeding
Groups. Chance plainly was
A factor but what else drove
Our ancestors to breed, develop
And fill the earth. Many forces
Were at play including the genes.

Darwin discovered evolution, chance
And natural selection. Much later
With the aid of a curious monk
We discovered the genetic system and
Then the double helix, the process

By which genes are exchanged from generation
To generation, each one of us, a new
Combination of inheritance from our
Ancestors. The genetic system is
An information code, a small computer
Which sends out proteins to build
From tiny cells each individual's well
Structured body, brain and driving force,
An engine well designed to direct
Each body's growth and structure
And to pass the ancestral design
Down through generations but
Always with variations from
Combining ancestral genes, from
Mistakes in transmission and from
Random mutation thereby allowing
Life to proliferate and survive
The clash of mighty systems, such
As plate tectonics, climate and asteroids.

Chance is a factor as Darwin discovered
In the amazing development of life.
The genetic system, however, is
An ingenious engine driving the
Marvelous proliferation of life over
The ages from tiny cells to dinosaurs,
To birds, to mammals and onward
To humans and perhaps beyond.
One can recognize intelligent design,
The brilliance of a marvelous plan with
Chance as a chosen tool to provide
Flexibility, survivability, and ultimately
Participation by intelligent beings acting
Freely to aid in their own and the world's
Creation

Enjoying a Rainy Day

In midafternoon the rain stopped
And the lake community came to life.
Outside the cottage door a chipping
Sparrow sang its beautiful song
Spotted with occasional bell-like
Tones; down the lake roared
A boat or two disturbing the quiet.
I was enticed into a long walk.
Song sparrows with their speckled
Chests decorated the bushes and
Entertained with their bubbling songs.
The lawns were crowded with red winged
Blackbirds and grackles with a young
One or two looking to be fed. A
Workman greeted me as he emerged
From shelter to continue constructing a
Cottage but thunder rumbled in
The hills and I returned to
The quiet cottage to relax and
Enjoy the next rainstorm and
Watch the raindrops bouncing on
The lake.

Biblical Promises

On Mondays I visit
Arthur Phillips' wife
Mary at the Jewish
Home for the aged.
As I left the building
I encountered an old
Student who remembered
My course in Commercial
Transactions. He is now
A Rabbi and teaching
A course for the elderly.
The book he uses is
Abraham's Children talking
About the source of
Many religions all influenced
By Abraham, whom God
Designated as the Father
Of many nations and children,
A blessing to the generations.

David the king once upon
A time proposed to build
A House for the Lord, a
Splendid Temple in Jerusalem.
Through the prophet Nathan,
God said: you shall not
Build a house for Me, I
Shall build a house for you.
Your son shall succeed to
Your throne and for all
Generations a king from the

House of David shall sit
On your throne. Was
That an empty promise?

The Lord Jesus born into
The House of David fulfills
The promises throughout
The Bible. For all generations
He sits on the throne of David
And makes Abraham a
Blessing to the Gentiles.

Moses said—the Lord your
God will raise up a
Leader like me and Him
You must follow and
The Lord Jesus leads His
People from all nations
Toward the Lord God
Reestablishing the Kingdom
Of God the Father as
Intended from the beginning.

Reading the Bible

When you read the Bible
Read it backwards or
Rather when you think
About the Bible think
About it backwards.
The Gospels are the culmination
Of a long story written
Episode by episode by
Those engaged in the struggle
In language, form and style
Understandable by the people
Of the time, a long story
Of the two thousand year
Struggle of a people to
Relate to their God, to
Wrestle like Jacob with
Their God or seen from a
Different perspective a long
Effort by God to relate to
And mold his people., to
Shape them as a potter
Shapes the clay. The gospels
At the end of that two thousand
Year wrestling match cap
The story. That long history
Can be understood in light
Of the Gospels, otherwise
It is a story of futility.

Emerging from History

Rabbis, according to Jewish
Legend, once were arguing.
In the midst of the heated
Exchange one rabbi called
On God to witness the merit
Of his position. In response
The heavens rolled with thunder.
The other rabbis claimed this
Was inappropriate and unfair.
If God wants to participate
Let Him come down and join
The argument, exchanging thought
With us, they reasonably claimed.

From time to time in the long
History of that struggle those
In desperate circumstances or
Those who love God cry out
For Him to rend the heavens
And come out of the mists to
Rescue and appear to His
Struggling people and as the
Story goes from age to age
God speaks in varied forms.
From a burning bush God
Spoke to a shoeless Moses.
In a whisper God appeared
On a mountain to Elijah.
The spirit of God rested upon
Many a prophet who then
Proclaimed: thus says the Lord.

From age to age God spoke
To his people and rescued them
In Egypt, for example, or in
The great return from Babylon.

At the end of the story, two
Thousand years from the time
Of Abraham God spoke through
The prophet John and then
Through His Son, the strap of Whose
Sandals, as John said, he was
Unworthy to loose. God
Appeared among His people,
Came down and joined the argument,
Rended the heavens and led the charge
To rescue a holy people from Rome
And local corruption and ineptitude,
Not with the sword but with love
And courage confronting and conquering
The oppressor over a three hundred
Year period of struggling and growing
Faith as the blessings of Abraham
Were extended to the Gentiles.

When you read the story backwards
It all makes sense, a story
Of a people relating to God
Wrestling from age to age
Developing, changing, understanding,
Becoming ready to extend
Their blessings to the world
While the Divine potter spun
And shaped and intervened
In one long continuing dialogue
And then appeared to take part

In the struggle, the argument,
The shaping and to lead the
Remaining stages, to attack
Oppression and substitute love.
When you read the story
Backwards it all hangs together
And the appearance of God
Among His people fits a
Two thousand year history
Of development, dialogue, struggle
And change.

God Speaks

God has spoken over the ages
To many people, as one can
Discern from the insights
In their stories and teachings.
God spoke through His prophet
Dekahaweeda to the Haudenosaunee
Proclaiming peace under the white pine
And planting the notion of federalism which
Has proved fruitful in
Extending peace through the nations.

In the mists of time beyond
Recorded history God apparently
Spoke to a primitive Indo-
European people and as they
Spread across the map of Eurasia
Some insights remained and proved
Fruitful, the Roman love
Of family, for example,
The deep insight of the legendary
Druids now lost to history
But witnessed by the early
Irish saints and their flourishing
Ready adoption of Christianity.
Among the Eurasians most obviously
He spoke to the ancient Hindus
Spiritual insights which endure
In many ways over the ages even
Until today and are found
In many forms including the
Teachings of the Buddha.

But most clearly He spoke
To Abraham and his many
Descendants and showed His
Willingness to dwell with
His people in the tent, in
The Ark of the Covenant, and
Less willingly in the Temple.
You shall be my people
And I shall be your God.
More vividly than elsewhere
God revealed His presence
And love of human beings
To Abraham and his descendants,
Promising His blessings
Would extend to the Gentiles.
And when He dwelt among
His people as the Christ
He instructed His disciples
To preach the Gospel to
All nations baptizing them
In the name of the Father,
The Son and the Holy Spirit.

Hear O Israel

Hear O Israel, the Lord
Your God is one God
And you shall love
The Lord, your God with
Your whole heart and soul.
The mark of the One God
Is love. Love is the essence
Of God. Within the One
God is relationship as
Revealed through the Christ
And recorded in the great
Insights of the Nicene Creed,
God through His Christ,
God from God, true God
From true God, of one substance
With the Father, came down
And dwelt among us.

It only makes sense if
The Christ is God as
St. John's Gospel discerns,
"And the Word was made flesh
And dwelt among us".
Within God is relationship
And through the Holy Spirit
We are invited into that
Relationship and even here
God dwells within us.
The essence of God is love
And we are invited into
That love.

Love and Not Tears

If God has joined us here
If He has pitched His tent
Among us, If He went before
Our ancestors in the Faith
In a pillar of fire by night
And revealed His presence
In the Temple and the Ark
Of the Covenant. If He then
Joined us as the Christ
Participating in our sufferings,
Challenging our oppressors,
Cleansing an acceptable people
Generation after generation,
Leading us gently and sometimes
Not so gently in our co-creation,
Changing, developing, metamorphosing
Human culture, promoting love,
Freedom, concern for the poor,
Allowing us to cry out to Him
In the midst of our struggles
As one who has suffered and
Understands, then the world
Makes sense. Then love and
Not tears is at the heart of things.

Recognizing God

As I recognize the cardinal's
Whistle in the early morning
Or the song sparrow's bubbling
Trill while walking on a country
Road so I recognize you,
My God, as I gaze at the beauty
And intelligent order of the heavens.

When I read a book I recognize
The author's thought, when
I see a famous painting I
Recognize the desire to create
And share its beauty, so
In the heavens I see beauty,
Beauty which communicates from
Person to person, the beauty
Of sparkling intelligence in the
Order and design of the stars
In the wonders of an evolving
Changing universe now 13.7
Billion years old, expanding
Rapidly, evolving, governed
Throughout by scientific laws
Suited for the evolution of
Intelligent creatures who can
Share and understand the
Scientific laws in their
Intricacies and delight in
The continuing discovery and
Intellectual explore as one
Marvel after another unfolds.

As I gaze at the universe
I see a Person who wants
To share the delight of exploration
And discovery and who wants
Us to see beauty everywhere,
A person who delights in the
Dance of intelligence and the
Splendor of beauty and wants
To exchange that delight with
Intelligent creatures who can
Explore and understand an
Appreciate the beauty and wonder
Of it all.

Discerning God

With the aid of Newton's
Surveying tools, Einstein's relativity
And Hubble's measurements
It is modestly easy to discern
The wonder of God's intelligence
In the scientific laws that govern
The universe, its billions of
Galaxies and 13.7 billion years.
To perceive His love of beauty
Just look on a clear night.
Look out into the ages or
At least into our galaxy.

Recognizing God in the complexities
Of evolution is a murkier task.
But chance is an intelligently
Chosen tool and the genetic
System is a marvelous
Generator of information and
A wise means for proliferation
Of the species and the survival
Of life. Looking at spring
Migration, a product of the
Ice age and generations of
Development since the feathered
Dinosaurs, one can praise
The wisdom of God and His
Love of beauty found in bird
After bird arriving in spring.

Finding God in the Tragedy
And mayhem of human history
Is a murkier task by far.
Perhaps because our thought tends
To the precise and mathematical.
Abstract beauty is hard to discern
In the struggle and blood of
Humanity's cultural evolution.
A taste for heroic ballad,
For brave and tragic song can
Help until confronted with
Human death or the oppression
And sadness of the county jail.
Then only God can redeem our tears.

We have a story and for those
Who believe a living presence,
A story of God's concern for
Humanity, His desire to dwell
With us, to mold and Sheppard
His people, a story of God's
Presence in age after age
From Abraham to the Christ
And then beyond as saints

Tell His story and perform
His work visiting the sick
And those in jail, feeding the
Hungry, rescuing the poor.
We have the story of the Christ
Sharing our sufferings, and
Carrying our burdens, challenging
Oppression, restarting our
Cultural evolution, our self-creation,
Allowing the poor to cry out

To one who hears and understands.
The story of the Christ in the
Tragedy and glory of human history
This story fits our circumstances.

Recognition: A Prelude to Love

Recognition can be a prelude
To the commitment of faith and love.
Recognition can grow and deepen
Over time beginning with a
Sudden flash of insight and wonder.
When recognition fits well with
Other experiences, with other things
We know then it is worth
Pursuing, experimenting to see
Whether it will deepen into a
Relationship. "Where do you"
Live Rabbi, the first disciples
Asked Jesus. Come and see He
Replied and they did and
Eventually preached the Gospel
And died for their love of
The Christ.

The Centerpiece

In the falling confetti
And debris of human history
In the muddle of our world
With its tragedies; war
And death, with its joys
And reconciliations, with its
Love and commitment, this
Story, the story of the Christ,
A story emerging from the long
Relation and struggle of God
With a people and continuing
Throughout history to the present,
This story of God dwelling
With His people, this story
Of the Christ is the piece
Of red confetti, the focal
Point, the jigsaw piece
Which fits the puzzle.

Harvest
Two Harvest Poems

"We'll All Go Together"

I.
Praise to you, my gracious Lord and God
For corn on tables and in the fields
Waving tall and green from farm to farm
Praise to You, my gracious Lord and God
For apples reddening, waiting the basket
For cider flowing from cider mills
Praise to You, my gracious Lord and God
For summer ripening into fall
For work awaiting in schools and fields
Praise to You, my gracious Lord and God
For woodland walks and summer recreation
For warm refreshing days and no disasters

Praise to You, my gracious Lord and God
For making us co-creators of this world
For joining us in that co-creation
Praise to You, my gracious Lord and God
For leading us in fields and harvest work
For joining in our sweat and tears.

II

Now let us join the Harvest crew
And work the fields together
Whether we began at the dawn of day
Or as the evening sun declines.
A whiff of fall is in the air
The corn is growing tall and strong
As apples redden on the trees.
For friendship, then, will you join with us.
Will you go along with us and
Work the fields together?
Will you go?

FINDING THE PRESENCE OF GOD:
A Critical and Explanatory Essay

Poetry, I am told should stand on its own without an explanation. Go back, then, and read the poems again. You do not have to read this explanatory essay. Rather than read this essay read the poetry again.

Poetry at times has the capability of allowing us to see what we might not otherwise perceive. To put it in other words, sometimes poetry provides insights which could be described as sudden perceptions of new patterns in the data. The hope of finding new insights is one reason why we read poetry.

When we acquire new insights we often want to inquire further. New insights require a setting, relationship with connected insights and sometimes qualification or further explanation. Poetry usually is not ideally suited to provide that additional background. This brief explanatory essay is designed to serve that function.

The Many Languages of Poetry

As a boy, Seamus Heaney grew up in County Derry, Northern Ireland. During the Second World War before he could read he would listen to an old fashioned radio in the isolation of his country farmhouse. All around him in his family with his siblings he would hear people talking English with an Irish accent. On the radio, however, he would hear a BBC announcer describing the war in a crisp probably south of England accent. The announcer would tell of bombing raids and battles across Europe perhaps at times using French, German or Italian words. When Seamus Heaney in Sweden accepted the Nobel prize for poetry, he gave a speech, The Nobel Lecture entitled Crediting Poetry(Heaney 1999 at 418), in which he described his early experience of hearing more than one language and becoming vaguely aware of the many communities in the world.

He explained:

> "The child in the bedroom listening simultaneously to the domestic idiom of his Irish home and the official idioms of the British broadcaster while picking up from behind both the signals of some other distress, that child was already being schooled for the complexities of his adult predicament, a future where he would have to adjudicate among promptings variously ethical, aesthetical, moral, political, metrical, skeptical, cultural, topical, typically post-colonial and, taken all together, simply impossible." (Heaney 1999 at 418).

Poetry, itself, written or sung, since our earliest civilizations and probably before, appears not only in many tongues but in multiple forms and structures with many purposes and functions. Read a few of Seamus Heaney's poems, for example, and see their different structures and then his great translation of the epic story of Beowulf. That one I seriously recommend for an entertaining weekend, especially if you haven't read it yet.

The poetry in these two volumes was written in the early twenty-first century at the beginning of my old age. Contrary to much twentieth century poetry it is plain spoken and straight forward. In that respect it is influenced by the Irish poets including Seamus Heaney but perhaps even more by Robert Frost. Once upon time poetry imitated song and was meant to be sung or read aloud. We may be returning to that with the poetry slams. But as a result of most of our twentieth century poetry we now usually think of reading poems to ourselves rather than reciting. Poems are a style of short essay designed to set forth brief thoughts, interesting insights, metaphors, images or pictures. The poems in these two volumes largely follow that pattern.

Poems in that pattern are able to explore ideas, a break with some poetic traditions, and I hope, provide insight into some complex questions. Poems as short essays exploring ideas while searching for insights follow an ancient tradition of didactic poetry. A good example of that, worth reading, can be found in the Hebrew Bible in the writings of Yeshua ben Sirach. Following that example you could characterize these two volumes of poetry and this essay as constituting a book of wisdom in the tradition of ben Sirach.

On the other hand, some of the poems in these two volumes are worth reading aloud. You may want to alter your pace from poem to poem or even within a poem. Some of the poems work best with a slow pace and some with an increasingly faster pace as the reading proceeds. From poem to poem you may want to experiment with the pace of recitation. Nevertheless, I am convinced that reading these volumes, one a night, straight through is the best way to appreciate this work which was designed as a unit.

The Many Disciplines in Academia

As a young man listening to the radio Seamus Heaney could be described as encountering the phenomenon of horizons. Horizons is a word used by some philosophers, Martin Heidegger, Hans Georg Gadamer and Bernard Lonergan, to symbolize the basic human situation of having limited knowledge and understanding. In a typical university as in life we encounter many horizons. However, well read a professor is he or she tends to be interested in and to see life and its problems most clearly in the context of his or her discipline.

In the physical world our vision is limited by the physical horizon, that circle where the sky and the earth or perhaps tall buildings meet. We know we can cross horizons. I can leave my home and travel to the family cottage on Erieville Reservoir. When I do that my vision and my mood change considerably.

In the intellectual sphere we also can cross horizons. It is possible to leave college and go to law school or to pursue a Ph.D. in physics. Those two routes establish two alternate intellectual horizons which a college student can cross into. It would be a little more difficult for a law professor or a professor of physics to cross into the alternate horizon. One can, however, accomplish that change of horizon simply by walking across the campus and taking courses in the other school or department.

The multiple disciplines and multiple horizons within a university are a substantial barrier to intellectual exchange and conversation both in academia and in our society. Both within the university and beyond we have multiple other horizons established by our different religious and political views and our many ethnic backgrounds.

In recent years, that is, the years just before and during the writing of these two volumes of poetry, there has been an on going clash between some religious views and the views of the scientific community. One function of these poems is to explore and provide some possible insights which you may find helpful in thinking about or perhaps resolving that dispute.

Sorting out Our World

Having enjoyed many children and grandchildren I find the development of a young child fascinating. That development takes place usually in the context of a loving family, that is, in an atmosphere of interpersonal relations. On many occasions I have thrown gently or handed a ball to a young person while saying "ball" over and over. I also have noticed the joy of the young one over a new achievement or a new insight as he or she begins to add pieces to his or her understanding of the world.

Martin Heidegger refers to the phenomenon just described as being thrown into a world. The child then begins sorting out that world in an effort to understand it. We all have had that experience and have replicated it on various occasions as we grow older. A college student newly arrived at a university, a foreign traveler in a new country, a graduate student entering an advanced field of study all find themselves in a new world, bewildering at first, which needs to be sorted out. Elsewhere I have described an experienced lawyer newly appointed as a judge as being thrown into a world which resembles to some extent his early experiences in law school.(Donnelly 2003). Often a new judge will joyfully and with enthusiasm embark on the task of sorting out that new world. The concept of being thrown into and sorting out a new world resembles to some extent and overlaps the concept of horizons discussed above.

Horizons in our modern world are established at times by sophisticated methodologies. Some advanced disciplines employ highly specialized methods, for example the scientific method, the analytical methods of economists, or the quasi-scientific methods of the social sciences. Other specialized methods such as history or law could be described as using a sophisticated specialized common sense method.

One definition of common sense would be the self-correcting process of learning through living. A young child learns to walk, talk and relate to the persons around her by an informal quasi empirical method of trial and error, that is, the self correcting process of learning through living. Most of our basic knowledge and skills are acquired by that means. We learn the basic facts about the world, how to swim, ride a bicycle and most importantly how to get along with friends, neighbors and colleagues by that common sense method.

Usually by the time we reach high school we begin to acquire skill in highly specialized non-common sense methods such as science, mathematics and perhaps logic or the social sciences. Geometry introduces us not only to a higher form of mathematics but also to logic. We continue to learn many things by common sense.

Poetry along with law, history and theology could be classified as a specialized sophisticated common sense method of understanding. If we lived a thousand years ago common sense would be our principal tool for understanding the world and in that context it would have serious limitations. When we use our basic common sense we often have difficulty getting beyond our horizons. I would argue, however, that during the past thousand years our common sense has become much more sophisticated. During that time the highly specialized methodologies such as science, mathematics logic, economics and the like have grown in power and perception. At the same time those disciplines have expanded our general knowledge and understanding. They have contributed to making our common sense more sophisticated. Our common sense knowledge has expanded with on-going input from the highly specialized disciplines. Also we are acquainted with those disciplines and what they can accomplish or discover. We can seek input from them when we have a difficult common sense decision to make. The sophisticated specialized common sense disciplines can do this systematically.

Most of our day to day activities continue to be conducted using our common sense but often with input from the highly specialized disciplines. We would no longer make the classic common sense mistake of believing that the sun goes around the earth. However, we are prone to what I perceive as a serious mistake in an opposite direction. A judge making an important legal decision could rely primarily on input from the sciences or economics as the foundation for his conclusion. In my view his decision ought to be grounded primarily in the sophisticated specialized common sense of his discipline which should have a place for input from the sciences and economics. To make the same point more clearly and dramatically by offering a caricature, imagine a young man or woman who uses science in an effort to find the perfect person to marry. While science may make a contribution to such a decision it cannot provide the basic foundation for it. We acquire our understanding of persons and our relationships with them over a lifetime by experience. That experience is the self correcting processes of learning through living. Common sense as so defined is the foundation for our understanding of personal relations. Sociology and psychology can help inform that common sense understanding but should never be a substitute for it.

Recognition

Several of the poems use the concept, "Recognition". Recognition is a form of insight employed in interpersonal relations. Recognition is what occurs when one says "my wife is good, not beautiful but good, although she may be beautiful also". It is a high point in interpersonal relations which can make the whole of life seem worthwhile.

Insight is a term employed by the philosopher-theologian, Bernard Lonergan primarily in his philosophical work, "Insight". (Lonergan 1970). If you have had some philosophy and are feeling intellectually acute you should read Insight. It may require some persistence. Otherwise somewhere in college or after you may want to read Lonergan's Method in Theology (Lonergan 1973), which is written more clearly and reads more smoothly. Method in Theology could provide you with an introduction to the study of intellectual method and to an understanding of insight. An insight as Lonergan uses that term is a sudden perception of a new pattern in the data. A scientist working on a problem in the course of his experiments suddenly may perceive a new way of organizing the facts he is developing. A lawyer working on an argument to be presented in court may perceive the way to persuade the judge and win the case. A poet may find the expression or image which will make the poem he is working on exciting. Insights are fundamental building blocks of knowledge and understanding in all intellectual endeavors. A friend of mine, David Granfield, who also was interested in Lonergan once noted, however, that an insight "is a bright idea, a snap judgment, a shrewd guess, a tentative understanding". He added: "It is like love at first sight, perhaps an infatuation but perhaps the beginning of a lifelong commitment."(Granfield 1988 at 3-6). Lonergan would describe a theory as a series of connected insights. A scientific theory in normal understanding requires verification. Actually scientists rather insist that theories be stated in a form that is falsifiable. Insights in all fields if we want to seriously pursue them should be checked out in some way.

One of our basic human abilities is to perceive patterns everywhere.

Often those perceptions are correct. The Poem, Woodpeckers, describes our ability to find patterns in woodpeckers (also in other birds and animals) based on taxonomy, the art of classification of animals using the study of physical features. Often enough, as the poem notes, those classifications are correct, and will predict what DNA will find. In other words the detection of patterns in the physical features of birds and animals can help us understand their evolution.

Scientists correctly note, however, that we often perceive fantastical patterns even when we are not writing science fiction. How do we control that inclination to fantasy and distinguish it from reality? Scientific method properly seeks to do that by adhering to the criteria of that method, by stating theories in falsifiable form, by seeking to verify or falsify those theories, by insisting on the consensus of the scientific community and on peer review. The careful, even plodding use of scientific method has produced great achievements and has advanced immensely our understanding of our universe.

However, scientific verification does not work in all fields. Important propositions cannot always be stated in falsifiable form. A general planning a military campaign can state his strategy in falsifiable form and ultimately his insight into the way to win an approaching battle will be verified or falsified. Verification, however, will come too late to affect the planning process. Likewise falsification will be a disaster which will come too late to benefit the planning of strategy.

In law we often need to interpret abstract concepts which state very important political or ethical propositions. An example would be the equal protection clause of the fourteenth amendment to the United States Constitution. Empirical studies can be helpful as indeed they were in *Brown v. Board of Education of Topeka Kansas*, the great school desegregation decision of the Warren Court. But empirical studies cannot settle the meaning of great ethical or political concepts. Again courts and lawyers have to make serious decisions without relying on scientific method.

That is a path we all have to follow and always have had to. Scientific method is not terribly helpful in choosing a career or in deciding whom to marry. Experience is relevant and wise advice from those with experience can be very helpful. Hopefully as we grow in age we also grow in wisdom. The poem entitled Wisdom offers an analysis of that great virtue. Wisdom is experienced understanding of how to do things, of craftsmanship. By analogy wisdom gives us an understanding of the practical art of relating to persons. Experience is an important ingredient in developing wisdom but wisdom is essentially a practical art, an understanding of how to do. Wisdom will employ science but is not a scientific discipline. Nevertheless wisdom appears to be very important to human survival. Indeed wisdom could be described as the experienced understanding of how to live our life. Science offers us a model of a rigorous and organized method which has a strong record of success in developing our knowledge of the physical universe. The scientific method, however, does not appear to be helpful when addressing a variety of important problems. One set of these problems are those dealing with interpersonal relations, with values and with recognition of another as a person who is to be respected and valued. Wisdom and insight are important to the recognition and understanding of persons, human relations and values.

Because we tend to become enmeshed in our horizons some scientists would argue that only propositions tested by the scientific method should be described as knowledge or truth. Those same scientists may regard beauty, music, values and love as important but as more ephemeral and not related to our search for reliable and trustworthy truth. Others would say that relationship between persons, values, love and beauty are among the most important aspects of life and deeply related to our search for truth and meaning.

Recognition, then, is a form of insight employed in interpersonal relations: it is a high point in our search for truth and meaning. Recognizing another as a person worthy of respect, concern and love is at the heart of our understanding of meaning and value.

One cannot verify recognition but one nevertheless can check it out. Does our recognition of a friend as good fit with our knowledge of him or her, with our continuing relationship and with her deeds? As recognition interplays with our developing values does it fit with our growing understanding of the world, with our experiences of persons and with our search for truth and meaning? Checking out for fit is not verification or falsification as scientists use those terms. Nevertheless it guards us against fantasy and can if we wish be conducted with significant rigor.

Beauty

Gerard Manley Hopkins who is one of my favorite poets describes the world as charged with the grandeur of God. I see the world as constantly and repeatedly beautiful. From sunset to the evening sky to the bird singing at dawn, from rose gardens in Oregon to walks along the Erie Canal with orioles flying across the water and ospreys plunging into its waves beauty is everywhere. The world is charged with the beauty of God.

Bringing analysis to bear on beauty, however, presents a complex picture. Visual beauty depends to a large extent upon light which itself is a complex phenomenon. Early in the twentieth century scientists began to perceive light both as a wave and as particles known as photons. The heat of a fireplace can produce light, that is a stream of photons released as electrons in the wood move more rapidly which is what we mean by heat. Electrons moving through a light bulb produce a similar effect. Most of our light comes from the sun and is generated in the heat of that atomic furnace.

In a rainbow or a prism light is broken down into a variety of colors which are the appearance of light moving at different wavelengths. Trees, flowers, sky and different colored houses reflect light moving on various wavelengths or absorb some of it allowing us to see a portion of the spectrum.

Our eyes have evolved to enable us to see certain wavelengths of light. Birds and other animals will see different portions of the spectrum perceiving light differently than we do. Eyes began to evolve long before the late Pre Cambrian period beginning as eye spots which could barely detect light. In the late Pre Cambrian and Cambrian era about 500 million years ago and later, there was an explosion of varied life forms many with eyes. It has been argued that the evolution of the eye caused the Cambrian explosion of life as organisms changed in response to the now greater capacity of predators or prey. Eyes have continued to evolve since the Cambrian explosion leading to the different visual capabilities of various birds, animals and ourselves.

After light reaches our eyes, further steps are necessary to allow us to perceive beauty. The images transmitted to eyes by reflected light must be impressed upon the eye and conveyed to our brains. The coordinated working of various parts of the brain then produces the mental image we are acquainted with and at times can recall that image from memory.

The perception of beauty then is a complex process with roots deep in the history of evolution as well as in the development of light, heat and the refraction of colors. Yet we perceive beauty everywhere.

We are familiar with the process of creating beauty because we ourselves are artists. From the time of the cave paintings in the vicinity of 40,000 B.C., humans have created beautiful images. We create beauty for ourselves in our houses and gardens. Normally, however, an artist wants to convey beauty to others. A painter usually paints his picture for others to see and enjoy.

In our understanding then beauty is created by a person for other persons to enjoy. Beauty is a form of communication and is designed to enhance the pleasure of others. The beauty we perceive everywhere in the universe is developed in complex ways. While that beauty is everywhere it is at least conceptually separable from the various structures we encounter in the world. Beauty as one the poems states is gratuitously added for us to enjoy. The gratuitousness of beauty coupled with its pervasive presence in the universe supports our recognition that the thoughtful work of a person lies behind that presence of beauty everywhere, a person who wants to enhance our pleasure and to share pleasure with us, to communicate by this means with us.

This understanding and analysis of beauty concluding in the perception of a Person is an example of what I mean by recognition. Recognition is not the result of scientific reasoning. Among other variances there is no way to verify or falsify the perception that a Person with an enormous appreciation of beauty is present in the universe.

Yet that perception is reinforced by finding beauty in other aspects of the universe than the visual. Music both man made and in the song of birds is beautiful. That beauty requires a different analysis than that offered for visual beauty although there are similarities. Try doing that analysis; you may find it interesting. We also find beauty in mathematical and scientific reasoning and in literature including poetry. When we find beauty in differing aspects of the universe and find our analysis of it converging that is confirmation of our original perception, our original insight or recognition. We discover that our recognition has the virtue of fit. That is a form of checking out although it is not verification and therefore not science. We may describe it as an aspect of wisdom.

Cosmology—Understanding the Universe

During the twentieth century a remarkable convergence occurred between science and religion. The Bible in the Book of Genesis describes our world as created by God. Therefore those who believe the Bible always have thought of the world as having a definite beginning. Likewise in the Gospels and other New Testament readings we find discussion of the Last Judgment. Christians therefore recognize a definite end for our world, at least for this earth. Learned discussions outside of religion, perhaps scientific, have not always perceived a beginning and an end for the world. Now, however, we know that at some point our sun will exhaust its atomic fuel bringing a definite end to our earth and the solar system as we know it.

Scientists during the mid and late twentieth century came to agree that our universe as we know it began with what is described as the Big Bang. The foundations for conceiving and developing a theory for the Big Bang began with the work of Edwin Hubble.

In the early twentieth century, scientists imagined that our Milky Way Galaxy was the entirety of a largely static universe. When Albert Einstein developed his theory of general relativity he found that his equations predicated an expanding universe. Unwilling to accept that, he added a "cosmological constant" to his theory as a correction which would preserve a static universe.

In the meantime Edwin Hubble, then an assistant astronomer who had just returned as a major from service in the First World War began his observations in California using the new Hooker Telescope. Focusing on the Andromeda nebula which contained a supervova, he calculated its distance at one million light years well beyond the 300,000 light years width that had been calculated for the Milky Way. Ultimately he concluded that the Andromeda nebula was a separate galaxy with millions of stars. With the Hooker telescope one could observe about seventy-five million nebulae, each one apparently an independent galaxy.

Further observations led to the conclusion that the galaxies were moving rapidly away; the universe was expanding. Einstein congratulated Hubble and then characterized as his greatest mistake his effort to preserve the static nature of the universe by his inclusion of the cosmological constant in his theory of general relativity.

Current theorists and cosmologists, however, use the cosmological constant as part of inflation theory.

In 1927 George Lemaitre, a Belgian astronomer and priest, proposed a theory that the universe developed from a primordial atom, a theory which eventually was molded into the multiple versions of big bang theory. To put it in contemporary terms our expanding universe began as a singularity, in some ways resembling a black hole, a point of intense gravitation and enormous but compact mass. Following something like an explosion there was, in modern thought, a period of rapid inflation. The 1965 discovery of "cosmic background radiation" provided sufficient verification of big bang theory to lead to its general acceptance in the scientific community.

Major events in a current timeline for the history of the universe would be: the big bang, approximately 13.7 billion years ago, followed by rapid inflation which may have lasted for a trillionth of a second, the development of subatomic particles called quarks, of protons and neutrons during the next fraction of a second, and then the formation of simple atoms of helium and hydrogen. The first stars, which could be described as a first generation formed out of swirling clouds of cosmic dust, under the pressure of gravity about two hundred and seventy five million years after the big bang. About a billion years after that explosion again under the pressure of gravity galaxies formed. When those early stars exploded into supernova, new elements eventually the entire periodic table were spilled out into the swirling cosmic dust where second and third generation stars were formed. Our sun is a third generation star approximately four billion years old.

Remarkably our expanding 13.7 billion year old universe developed over that long expanse of time in ways necessary to the evolution of life. The first and second generation stars manufactured the carbon atoms foundational for carbon based life. The strong force was strong enough to allow the formation of the stars. Gravity was weak enough to allow stars to endure for billions of years rather than rapidly burning out. The entire universe appears to be governed by the same set of scientific laws.

Stepping back from and contemplating that scientific account of the development of our universe we again can recognize the presence of a Person. Newton, Einstein, Hubble and others have developed remarkable theories setting forth the structure of our universe and the scientific laws governing it. These laws appear to be pervasive throughout an enormous universe with billions of galaxies. Everything we know, all our experiences, leads us to perceive intelligence behind those scientific laws. Intelligence as we know it is a mark of a person. There appears to be a person of great intelligence and power behind the development of the universe and its scientific laws.

Consider now what cosmologists call the anthropic principle. As the poem, Troublesome, points out: Here we are an intelligent species discovering the scientific laws which govern the universe. If we are here then the universe must be suitable for our evolution. Indeed the vast structures appear arranged, among other goals, to produce carbon based life such as ours. Several generations of stars were required to produce all the elements in the periodic table. Carbon in particular which is a foundation for our life form was manufactured by second or third generation stars.

From where we stand, from hindsight, it looks as if a Person of great power and intelligence structured our universe while desiring it to produce intelligent life which could discover, marvel at and contemplate the scientific laws which govern that universe.

When contemplating the pervasive beauty of our universe and our world, our earth, one can perceive the presence of a Person. Again as one recognizes a powerful and intelligent Person who developed our universe governed throughout by scientific laws, as one perceives a desire for intelligent life to contemplate the marvelous order of the universe there is convergence and fit. One can recognize convergence and fit. Here is a powerful and intelligent Person who loves beauty and wants to share beauty and intelligence with us.

Again, however, it is necessary to reiterate that this is not science and should not be taught as science. Rather this recognition is a work of wisdom, of that human and rational intelligence which allows us to understand our fellow human beings as persons and to develop relations with them.

There should be no scientific objections to that perception. Nevertheless some scientists or others who perceive themselves as skeptical would object. One objection develops from string theory. String theory is a current effort to reconcile Einstein's theory of general relativity with quantum mechanics, a truly worthwhile effort which would provide a new and more general foundation of theoretical physics. String theory speculates that there are more dimensions than the three, length, breadth and width or four if we add time as a dimension. String theory would perceive the possibility of five, ten or more dimensions. In a similar manner there may be multiple universes either preceding the big bang or developing simultaneously with it. I find string theory fascinating and I am inclined to think there may be a number of universes.

Skeptics, however, argue that there may be millions, perhaps billions of universes all governed by different laws, some rational, some perhaps amazingly irrational. Our universe, then, is accidentally the product of chance. If the operating forces produce enough universes, one of them by chance may be governed throughout by the same scientific laws and may be suited for the evolution of intelligent beings.

This theory has some resemblance to the notion that a million monkeys typing randomly on a million typewriters would eventually produce all the literature that has been written including the poetry in this book and the vastly better poetry of William Shakespeare.

One should note that these notions not only are speculative but appear to violate Occam's razor. That rule of art in the construction of scientific theories states that one should not multiply entities unnecessarily.

There is some resemblance between these speculative theories of skeptics and a traditional philosophic move. Philosophers desiring and searching for absolute certainty wanted a totally clear and certain starting point for their philosophic reasoning. See for example the work of Rene' Descartes. Idealists would deny the existence of other persons and the external world because what is outside our mind may be an illusion, perhaps the work of a fabulous and wicked monster. I would conclude that the idealist problems are simply the product of a mistaken method. In our reasoning we should not worry about delusions created by fabulous monsters.

Likewise when we recognize the presence or goodness of a person we should not require ourselves to refute all possible speculative theories. When I recognize that my wife is good I should not worry that this appearance is a delusion of a fabulous monster.

A more serious scientific objection is that there is no way to verify that an intelligent person is the source of scientific laws which govern our universe and that the conclusion that there is such a person is not stated in falsifiable form. That, however, is a requirement of scientific method. Human rationality is not restricted to science and its methods. That was discussed earlier in this essay. General intellectual method should ask for some form of checking out insights. A proposed form for the insight, I have called recognition, is fit. The convergence of beauty and intelligence in the universe is the beginning of fit.

Evolution

During the last century or two, the most serious clashes between science and religion have centered on the theory of evolution. In recent years some advocates of religion, sometimes described as fundamentalists have developed various theories of creationism, one of which is labeled a theory of intelligent design and is alleged to be a scientific theory which they argue should be taught in high school science classes. Many scientists reject vigorously the claim that intelligent design is a scientific theory and abhor the notion that it should be taught in high school science classes. A summary scientific history of evolution, which I support, would read as follows:

Four billion six hundred thousand years ago between nine and ten billion years after the big bang our sun and our solar system formed. Shortly after, as we can detect from tiny fossils, primitive life forms and viruses developed. For about two billion years life on earth would be represented primarily by small one cell organisms. Some of the early organisms, the ancestors of modern vegetation, used photosynthesis adding to the presence of oxygen in our atmosphere. Between one billion five hundred thousand years ago and the beginning of the Cambrian age about five hundred and forty-five million years ago more complex animals such as multicelled jellyfish like entities emerged. That age ended apparently with the first major extinction.

The Cambrian Age began with a great proliferation, known as the Cambrian explosion, of many new types of life including most of the major phyla. Perhaps the preceding extinction opened niches which the remaining life forms rapidly filled. Another possibility is that the evolution of eyes such as the new crystal eyes of the trilobites made hunters more powerful. Organisms, then, developed in response to new possibilities for successful survival. Other organisms in response survived because of the evolution of appropriate defense strategies.

The last of the trilobites vanished at the end of the Permian Age about two hundred and fifty million years ago. The mass extinction at the end of the Permian Age apparently resulted from significant cooling of the world's climate, perhaps a major ice age. A great diversification of species followed including the evolution of the first dinosaurs. By the Cretaceous Age between one hundred and thirty and sixty-five billion years ago the dinosaurs reached the peak of their dominant development.

The age of dinosaurs came to a dramatic end sixty-five million years ago, most likely due to a large meteorite which crashed into the earth in the vicinity of the Mexican Yucatan Peninsula. The small mammals and primitive birds who survived were then free to proliferate to fill the vacant ecological niches. Eventually the primitive primates evolved into the great apes, the hominids and into human beings.

Charles Darwin announced his theory of natural selection in 1858. Natural Selection as Darwin explained it in the Origin of Species offers the struggle to survive and reproduce as a central mechanism for the evolution and proliferation of the world's multiple species which have evolved since the earth's beginning as one system. Ultimately humans and dinosaurs have common ancestors.

Natural selection always a remarkably good theory now is generally accepted among scientists as the explanation for the evolutionary development of the world's species. However in the twenty-first century natural selection can not be perceived as the only force at work in evolution. The changing environment particularly at the times when most extinctions occurred and the following opportunities for extensive proliferation to fill environmental niches were principal factors.

In Darwin's theory several factors were emphasized as important to understanding evolution. Natural selection, of course, was important. Darwin essentially argued that all of life was one system with bacteria and plants related to dinosaurs and humans. Chance was and continues to be a very important factor in Darwinian theory related, of course, to the process of Natural Selection. Subsequent developments in the history of genetics added a number of additional factors.

By 1900 Gregor Mendel's work on some basic laws of genetics was recognized. One of the poems describes Gregor Mendel as a curious monk which is accurate. While experimenting on pea plants Mendel discovered the laws of heredity. For example, factors which today we would call genes are passed to offspring in the course of reproduction. Dominant and recessive genes may be inherited. In hybrid pea plants such genes will produce a variegated pattern of inherited traits in subsequent generations.

In the nineteen twenties probing scientists began to focus on nucleic acid. By 1944 it was clear that genes consist of DNA, a molecule of nucleic acid, rather than proteins. In 1953 Watson and Crick discovered the double helix structure of DNA. By 1987 DNA could be used to identify a criminal suspect. Scientists then began to map the genome of various species and now have mapped the DNA structure of the human genome.

Using mitochondrial DNA scientists exploring human heredity now can trace modern human origins to a female ancestor in Africa more than 200,000 years ago. By now it is apparent that DNA is the vehicle for evolution. Steady mutations or genetic drift offer the possibility of change. Isolated members of species through genetic drift will change gradually into a subspecies. External forces such as the sudden availability (as in the Cambrian age) of multiple evolutionary niches or the plunging of an asteroid 65,000,000 years ago into the earth also will affect evolution. Chance and survivorability in the face of environmental change are important factors. DNA, however, is the vehicle for and the record of evolutionary change. Darwin was right, as DNA demonstrates, that in the biological life on the earth we are dealing with one system.

The Fundamentalist Response

A significant portion of Christian fundamentalists take the Bible literally. The modern use of form criticism to understand the structure and intent of biblical stories is not popular among Fundamentalists. Some fundamentalists, then, would claim that the account in Genesis of God's creation of the world is not a story told to primitive people to illustrate the presence of God in creation but literally true down to minute details. Six days means six days and not six ages of the world. When God created man from the slime of the earth that refers to mud or clay and not to creation through evolution over a 4 billion year period. Through a calculation of the periods of history and the generations referred to throughout the Bible some fundamentalists claim that the world is 6,000 to 10,000 years old. I would argue that this is a serious misreading and misinterpretation of the Bible.

The Creationist Theory of Intelligent Design argues that bird, animal and human structures are too complex to have evolved without the intervention of an intelligent designer. Some versions of intelligent design would recognize evolutionary change within a species to produce several subspecies but most versions insist that each species is separately created.

There are a series of difficulties with Creationist theories of intelligent design. One can start the list of difficulties with the serious misreading of the Bible followed by a disregard of a generally accepted scientific theory supported by extensive evidence and constant new discovery, the recent discovery, for example, of feathered dinosaurs in Chinese fossil deposits. From a scientific perspective an important flaw is the misrepresentation of Intelligent Design Theory as scientific theorizing. Intelligent Design Theory is not science. The statement that there is an intelligent designer is not verifiable and is not stated in falsifiable form.

A Role for Intelligent Design

The Creationist Theories of Intelligent Design are erroneous both in their serious misreading of the Bible and in their disregard of the generally accepted scientific discoveries regarding evolution. I would argue, as I have above, that they are not erroneous in perceiving intelligent design in the universe and the development of the many species on our earth. My argument again is not science but Interpretation developed with the assistance of Recognition. I find it very difficult not to recognize an intelligent Person who loves beauty behind the development and structure of our earth and our universe. As argued above, however, that interpretation must be consistent with the findings of science even though it goes beyond those findings.

In the early twenty-first century to support a perception that intelligence is at work throughout our universe and also in the evolution of the many species on earth one must account for the continuing presence of chance. During the eighteenth century the confrontation with chance, if it occurred, would have been shocking. During the twenty-first century we are more sophisticated. When we design complex artificial systems, for example advanced computer programs, we not only provide for the element of chance but often deliberately build chance into the system for the purpose of providing flexibility.

Chance, chaos theory, the uncertainty principle, the struggles of evolution, provide flexibility in the development of the universe. Statistical probability nevertheless can provide sufficient order to support a theory of intelligent design. Statistical probability coupled with the presence of chance can provide the necessary conditions for the side by side existence of human intelligence and human freedom. The flexibility provided by chance can preserve the possibility of intervention from time to time by a providential creator. The regular presence of chance in our universe is not inconsistent with a perception of intelligent design in that universe.

After an initial sorting through the perception of intelligent design in our universe does not seem to be out of accord with the data. It is a continuing perception over the ages although not one that can be scientifically verified. However, as we construct an interpretation of the universe we find ourselves in, intelligent design appears to be a valuable insight consistent with the data and capable of relation to other insights, to the perception of beauty, a necessarily interpersonal phenomenon appearing spectacularly over and over in the world in which we live.

Structures and Systems

The areas I know fondly as central and western New York, which others refer to as upstate, were seriously affected by the last great ice age. The territory surrounding Syracuse, New York where I teach at Syracuse University were covered by a mile high glacier 12,000 years ago. The many fascinating waterfalls in central and Western New York including Niagara Falls and our neighbor, the smaller but still dramatic Chittenango Falls, were all formed by the retreating glaciers of the last Ice Age.

About 20,000 years ago the glacier reached as far south as the present New York City. When the climate began to warm the glacier started to melt and slowly retreat to the north. At one point this frozen mass of ice was 5,000 to 7,000 feet high and covered the high mountains of New York's Adirondacks Park. As it melted vast quantities of water spread over the landscape. In the hills surrounding many valleys the water cascaded down carving gorges and forming waterfalls. When the ice melted around Niagara the whole backed up force of the great lakes began to pour over the falls into what is now Lake Ontario. In the early period of glacial melt the run off from the Great Lakes formed a much larger lake which geologists call Lake Iroquois.

The glaciers and the vast quantities of water from glacial melt transformed the landscape of New York State. For some time ice blocked the flow of water from Lake Iroquois into what is now the St. Lawrence River. Instead the waters from the lake and the melting glacier flowed south through old river beds which had been carved deeper by the glacier. The glacier had deposited piles of debris in the south as it retreated northwards. That debris blocked the flow of water and prevented the old rivers in Central and Western New York from being reestablished. Instead as they filled with water from the melting ice they became the Finger Lakes, Skaneateles, Cayuga, Seneca and the rest. Oneida Lake to the North of Syracuse runs in a different direction, east and west, than the north-south stretch of the Finger Lakes and has a different history. Oneida Lake is the remains in Central New York of Lake Iroquois.

Lake Iroquois originally emptied into what is now the Mohawk River and then on down through the Hudson to the ocean. When the glacial meltdown finally removed the ice dam from the eastern end of Lake Iroquois, the outflow of water from the Great Lakes changed direction and recreated the mighty St. Lawrence. The St. Lawrence River now flows from Lake Ontario through the Thousand Islands and along the border between New York and Canada on past Montreal, Quebec and the Gaspe Peninsula to the Atlantic Ocean. The St. Lawrence is the largest, most beautiful and most powerful river I have seen.

I remember my amazement when I first realized a number of years ago that the landscape of Central and Western New York had been reshaped, restructured and recreated in the last 12,000 years. I continue to be amazed.

The geological history of New York, however, is much more ancient than the reshaping of our landscape by the dramatic events accompanying the meltdown, 12,000 years ago of the last Ice Age. To understand the slow development over the ages of the landscape and geology of New York it is necessary to understand plate tectonics.

Only in the last half of the twentieth century did scientists begin to understand clearly and accept that the Earth's crust is divided between more than twelve moving plates (current estimate 6-7 large plates and about 14 smaller ones) which carry the continents and some of the ocean floor slowly from place to place. These plates are able to move because they float on a dense layer of rock which under high pressure and heat from the earth's interior behaves like plastic. Radioactive heat from the earth's interior provides the energy to move the continental plates.

Late in the Precambrian period about 650 million years ago the moving plates had the primitive continents or segments of them in a giant supercontinent which we call Rodinia. The plate carrying the sub-continent of India was located in the center of this supercontinent. What is now Antarctic bordered India and sat across the equator on the border of a prehistoric ocean. Laurentia, a name often used for the primitive beginnings of our North American continent, was part of a large foot which stuck out from the bottom of the supercontinent in the vicinity of the South Pole.

By the late Cambrian period about 514 million years ago, Rodinia, the supercontinent, had broken up and continental drift had scattered its pieces. Laurentia, the primitive continent on the North American continental plate, sat by itself across the equator. What is now New York faced south across a narrow ocean towards a small continent called Baltica which itself was a short distance from the South Pole.

Laurentia at that time was a barren continent and much smaller than the current North America. The basic substructure of North America constructed above the continental plate from Precambrian rocks is called the Canadian Shield. The Canadian Shield layer of rocks underlies much of New York State. In the Cambrian period New York would have been covered by a shallow sea. Sediment from that sea began to form the shale and limestone which built the current landscape of New York over the substructure of the Canadian Shield.

In the Cambrian period there was an explosion of new forms of life. The shallow sea covering New York would have teamed with that new life. The sedimentary rocks formed at the bottom of that sea, the slates and limestone now covering Central New York, are full of the fossil remains of that sea life. Tribolites evolved in vast numbers and prolific forms during the Cambrian explosion. It is a delight to find their fossil remains in Central New York.

By 425 million years ago the continent of Baltica moving from the south had slammed into the side of Laurentia along what is now the east coast of the North American continent. Laurentia still was lying on its side across the equator. At first the incoming plate was thrust under the plate supporting Laurentia creating a number of offshore volcanic islands which eventually were shoved against and welded to the continent. As the incoming continent continued to shove, the ancestral Taconic Mountains were created. The new high mountains stretched along what is now the east coast of northern United States. Over the following ages these mountains eroded and the sediment from that erosion flowed towards what are now the western portions of New York filing in the shallow seas.

An appropriate image for the movement over the last 1,000,000,000 years of the continents and the tectonic plates on which they rest is the amusement park ride and game usually called bumper cars. One can imagine the continents over the ages playing an on-going game of bumper cars across the surface of the earth. As continents bump into each other again and again in a variety of ways and places mountains are raised or thrust up, magnum leaks through creaks creating granite cliffs; where plates are thrust under plates volcanoes erupt; volcanic islands crash into continents. Mountain ranges are created and then erode over the years filing in shallow seas with their debris as they disappear. Then new mountains are created and the process repeats. Over the last billion years through this process continents which originally were relatively small and covered by shallow seas grew in size. The landscape evolved from originally barren and plain formations to the presently fascinating structures. The continental game of bumper cars was a process for developing and structuring the continents.

By 306,000,000 years ago the drifting continents came together again to create the supercontinent called Pangaea. Africa and South America were jammed together. Antarctic was attached to the southern end of Africa. The subcontinent of India just north of Antarctica was jammed with Madagascar against the southeastern coast of Africa. North America was attached to parts of Europe and mountain ranges were created as their respective plates came together. One mountain range which still can be traced ran across portions of North America into England and across Northern Europe. By this time the North American continent stood upright north of the equator in a position somewhat resembling its present location.

During the Permian era (290 million to 250 million years ago) reptiles spread across the vast supercontinent. The vast forests of giant ferns which developed during the previous Carboniferous Era began to yield to gymnosperms. At the end of the Permian era a mass extinction bought an end to much of the marine life including the last of the trilobites.

Tracing similar trilobites fossils across continents is one way of determining where mountain ranges and continents were located. For example, similar tribolite remains can be found in Newfoundland and Wales demonstrating the connection during an earlier age between those areas.

The first dinosaurs and surprisingly the first mammals appeared during the next Triassic era (250 million to 190 million years ago) while the continents still clung to each other in Pangaea, the supercontinent. During the Jurassic period (190 million to 130 million years ago) while dinosaurs flourished and the first birds appeared Pangaea began to break apart. The dinosaurs reached their dominant peak during the Cretaceous age (130 million to 65 million years ago). Mammals, birds and flowering plants began to diversify. In the meantime Pangaea broke apart. By 94 million years ago there were separate continents in shapes resembling their current configuration. However, India remained off the coast of Africa near Madagascar. The Himalayas Mountains were not yet created. The Atlantic Ocean, North and South, was a narrow sea running between the Americas on the west and Europe and Africa on the east.

When the Cretaceous period closed dramatically 65 million years ago the continents appearing very modern still were closer and the Atlantic Ocean was narrower than now. India moving north was still south of Asia and not connected to it. The modern age of mammals and birds was beginning. The mass extinction of dinosaurs about 65 million years ago probably was caused by the impact of a large meteor or asteroid with the earth in the vicinity of the Yucatan peninsula near the Gulf of Mexico. India crashed into southern Asia beginning about 50 to 55 million years ago. The Himalayas began to rise as mammals began to flourish and widely diversify.

Please note that the geological structures of our earth are dynamic and that those dynamic structures created much of the continents and landscape that we see in our world today. The interlocking work of plate tectonics, volcanoes, erosion, shallow seas and sedimentary deposits is what I would call a system. It is like a system of machines and computers in a factory and like such a system it appears designed to manufacture the continents and landscape we know today and perhaps change them again in the future. The system just described interplays with other systems, for example, the climate. Climate as exemplified by the Ice Ages and the meltdown interplayed with geological history to create the landscape of Central and Western New York as we know them today.

Interpretation

When I contemplate the history of our universe from the big bang to our third generation star, the sun, and our solar system, I perceive, as described earlier, the work of an intelligent creator. I also perceive a system at work slowly from the first to the third generation stars producing the conditions necessary for the evolution of intelligent life. When I contemplate the development of our earth, the role of plate tectonics and related phenomenon interplaying with climate and all that goes with it, I perceive interlocking systems at work in a manner similar to the development of the stars and planets over three generations since the big bang. And again I perceive intelligent purposive design and recognize a powerful and intelligent Person at work. I perceive that intelligent Person as appropriately designing systems to do His work. And again I note that everything particularly the landscape of Central New York with its mountains, lakes and waterfalls is beautiful.

This perception and interpretation is not science although it is consistent with science. I would offer the possibility that the perception of systems at work interlocking with each other may be worth scientific investigation. Note that plate tectonics and climate are not the only systems working with each other. The operation of the genes, I would think also constitutes a system. The genetic system working through and with proteins manufacturers each human and animal body. The genetic system also provides diversification and survival. Each human and animal is unique because of the double helix and inheritance from both parents. Genes regularly mutate producing genetic drifts and the possibility of new species. As one of the poems explains the genetic system allows life to survive when large is good or when small is necessary.

During the history of evolution the genetic system interplays with climate, plate tectonics and asteroids to produce diverse species some of which survive. One should note that dinosaurs and mammals originated when the continents joined to form Pangaea. That supercontinent provided a platform allowing these developing species to spread across the earth. When Pangaea broke up after dinosaurs and mammals had spread across its landscape and many continents the conditions were established for further diversification through among other means isolated breeding groups.

Again I perceive intelligent design including a great and vast work of engineering to produce systems designed to perform productive works. As the poem, Systems, points out these interlocking feats of engineering are designed to produce something like the cardinal and the chimpanzee and, of course; intelligent life. As when one contemplates the history of our universe from the Big Bang to our solar system, it is hard to escape the perception of a powerful and intelligent Person at work.

Objections

To summarize the insights offered in the segment just above, I perceive a person of powerful intelligence at work in our universe and in the development of our earth. Our universe is governed throughout by the same scientific laws. The anthrophic principle is correct: not only is our universe suitable for the evolution of intelligent life, it appears to be designed to do that among other things. The elements necessary for the existence and flourishing of intelligent life are gradually manufactured by three generations of stars and exploding supernova and now despite that apparently haphazard development appear in logical order in the periodic table. Since the Big Bang one can perceive the universe as a gigantic task of celestial engineering. Not only is the universe governed throughout by scientific laws, it is regularly and repeatedly beautiful. In a universe suitable for the evolution of intelligent life it appears that the engineer and intelligent designer is inviting intelligent creatures to contemplate the scientific laws and to appreciate beauty found throughout. The intelligent designer apparently desires to communicate with us.

On earth I perceive a continuation of the same pattern. Again, giant well designed systems, plate tectonics, climate, asteroids from the solar system combine to structure and restructure our earth, to build continents and landscapes. Those systems interlock with the genetic system, again well designed and apparently purposive, to preserve and shape life, to proliferate the species. As the universe appears suitable for the evolution of intelligent life and since these interlocking systems on earth in fact produced intelligent life it seems they are part of a grand design planned for that purpose among others. Again scientific laws, including laws governing plate tectonics, climate and genetics, are pervasive. And again our earth is regularly and repeatedly beautiful.

Nevertheless, skeptics and others would disagree with and offer a number of objections to these conclusions. A basic objection which I agree with is that these conclusions are not science. These perceptions are not scientific because there is no way to verify that there is an intelligent designer at work in the universe and that conclusion is not stated in falsifiable form. The perception of a powerful and intelligent designer is a conclusion drawn from interpretation.

Other objectors would include an argument that the marvelous and dynamic structures of our universe all flowed automatically from the Big Bang, the structure of the subatomic particles and early atoms that emerged from that explosion and from the forces, the strong force, the weak force, gravity etc. which began to function at that moment of origin. Although my perception would be different, I am not seriously troubled by that observation. My difference with that perception begins with the lack of scientific evidence connecting the structure of atoms, subatomic particles and forces with plate tectonics. Rather it seems that as structures become more complex new scientific laws become effective and govern the new structures. I offer that possibility as an observation for investigation and discussion and not as a scientific conclusion. I also note a rather large role for chance which may be inconsistent with a chain of causation stretching back to the early forces and elements which emerged following the Big Bang. The large role of chance would allow periodic intervention by an intelligent designer.

Nevertheless, if it is demonstrated that all subsequent developments were predetermined by the events and structures immediately following the Big Bang, that would not be inconsistent with the perception of an intelligent designer. The perception of an intelligent designer as described above would remain. Only the manner in which that designer worked would change. It would require a remarkably powerful intelligence to arrange that flow of events, forces and developments predetermined at the moment of the Big Bang without further interference.

As Darwin argued evolution proceeds incrementally, step by step. The feathers on a feathered dinosaur are not designed for flight nor are they steps on the road towards song birds. Feathers continue as a feature of feathered dinosaurs because they offer some immediate advantage perhaps warmth. An intelligent designer arguably should proceed less indirectly. Creationists often claim that each species of bird and animal is individually created. That approach although inconsistent with the data would seem more compatible with the process of intelligent design than manufacturing evolution thorough great systems, plate tectonics, climate, and the genetic system as described above.

I would disagree and argue that the use of great systems to structure the world and manufacture evolution is compatible with intelligent design and may be the sensible way to proceed. It is more efficient, provides greater flexibility and ultimately is more compatible with freedom for intelligent creatures.

Some skeptical advocates of evolution would point to what they would call mistakes or unhappy moments in its history. The back problems we experience, for example, may be due to the adjustments our legs and back made when we started to walk erect after descending from trees to the African Savanah. If we were designed more carefully and perhaps more directly as a species those problems would not occur. For similar reasons it is more difficult for human mothers to deliver their children at the moment of birth than for female chimpanzees, our near evolutionary cousins. These mistakes, disadvantages, or undesirable structures, skeptics would argue are incompatible with intelligent design.

A similar objection with a more cutting edge would be that evolution is a cruel system and hence incompatible with the notion of a compassionate intelligent designer. That objection would be illustrated by natural selection, the survival of the fittest, the death and elimination of species such as tribolites, dinosaurs, saber tooth tigers, early species of humanoids, homo erectus, the Neanderthals, and others.

An answer to this set of objections requires a more complex analysis. To begin we obviously live in an imperfect world. It is not surprising then that occasionally the results of evolution would be imperfect. Reflecting on traditional religious concepts. I would note that only God is perfect. We, His creatures, then, are necessarily imperfect. If God created a perfect creature, that creature would be the equivalent of God and identical with Him. In Christian theology God the Father did generate a Person united with Him in the Trinity, namely God the Son. If out of love God wanted to create someone other than Himself, that person necessarily must be imperfect. The imperfection of our universe is inevitable.

Once we grant that our universe is imperfect and necessarily must be imperfect then the question becomes what sort and degree of imperfection will be present in our world. There is no reason to believe when all things are considered that our universe is more imperfect than some other more desirable universe.

The choice and use of great systems to manufacturer our earth and the creatures present on it when all things are considered may be the most desirable plan. Allowing chance to have a strong role insures flexibility and provides a foundation for human freedom. Chance and survivorablity may lead to evolutionary results which are desirable in the circumstances although there are downsides. Altogether the results of evolution are desirable.

It is interesting that some skeptics who support evolution are sufficiently critical of it to find that it is incompatible with the presence of a loving Creator. I would disagree and find that evolution is a magnificent tool of an intelligent and loving creator.

A final set of objections would contend that the reasoning supporting the perception of a powerful and intelligent designer of our universe and our earth is necessarily soft, speculative reasoning. For example, there is an enormous leap from the perception of a fellow human being whom we can see and talk to as a person to the conclusion that there is a person behind the intelligent design perceived in the universe.

In reply I would note that the sort of reasoning which leads to the perception of a powerful and intelligent Person who designed our universe and our earth is very similar to the process by which we perceive our fellow humans as persons. That perception is vital to human civilization. We treasure, for example, Thomas Jefferson's statement in the Declaration of Independence that "we hold these truths to be self-evident, that all men are created equal and are endowed by their creator with certain inalienable rights. Among these are the rights to life, liberty and the pursuit of happiness". To find an intelligent creator behind the scientific laws, the great systems and the beauty of the universe and our earth requires a reasoning process and perception somewhat different than the perception that my friend or my wife is good although the process is similar. Nevertheless the facts and impressions regarding the universe and its structures are present before us. When contemplating our universe leads us to recognize an intelligent and powerful creator we should not set aside that understanding because of a narrow view of intellectual method.

A Providential God

Up to now we have been concentrating on the confrontation between science and those religious thinkers who call themselves Creationists or advocates of Intelligent Design. Now I want to offer a suggestion that the more basic underlying quarrel is between those who perceive a Providential God who is concerned with His creatures on earth and responds to their prayers and those who reject that perception.

During the eighteenth century deists and others who adhered to a theory of a clock-maker God did so on the argument that the world governed by rigorous scientific laws was not open to supernatural interference. Indeed some would imagine a covenant by God not to disturb His scientific laws. Some in more recent years would testify as did Einstein to an almost mystical appreciation of an intelligent God behind the marvelous order of a universe governed throughout by scientific laws while insisting that such a God would not be concerned with minutia including the activities of creatures on a small planet on the edge of one galaxy. Skeptics regularly insist upon humility: science has demonstrated that our earth is not the center of our universe, that we as the product of evolution are not seriously different than our fellow mammals. A God, they insist, if He exists, would not be concerned with us.

The ancient pagan religions and some modern descendants offer stories of gods, some beneficent and some nasty, who regularly interfere in human affairs. Pagan religious then seek to relate to those gods, seek their help or avoid their ill will. The offering of prayers and sacrifices were a means of propitiating those gods. Perhaps those gods were personifications of the forces of nature.

The modern understanding of a providential God largely is the product of religions who claim descent from Abraham. Primarily these include Judaism, Christianity and Islam. We find the first portrait of a providential God in the Hebrew Bible beginning with the Torah, the first five books of that Bible.

Over the ages and at this moment in these United States many persons find God while regularly reading the Bible. I recommend it to you. Certainly read Genesis, Exodus and the Psalms. You may find the histories including the story of David beginning in the Book of Samuel interesting and perhaps fascinating reading. In the monasteries both ancient and more recent life revolves around chanting the psalms. During that exercise or following upon it monks regularly find their lives touched by an experience of God.

If you read the Bible straight through you may perceive it as a unit, as one great book. One can understand it as the story of a people, Israel, wrestling with God. Those who wrote it, however, did not write as a unit. As modern form criticism has revealed each segment of the Bible was written separately at different times and for different purposes. There are, for example, two creation stories in Genesis each written at different times and merged over the ages. The second creation story apparently was written during the Babylonian captivity to counter the Babylonian creation story. Under that story we were created from dragon's blood. The stories of Job and Jonah are fictional, small novels or long parables designed to illustrate and explore theological or moral points. The histories are history or legend but not written according to the criteria of modern historiography. When interpreting the Bible one ought to address each unit or part of a unit with consciousness of its form, functions and purpose.

Nevertheless, I would contend that it is appropriate to read the Bible and perceive it as a unit. The Bible is the product of a great culture. While it is not a modern work of history it is the story of that culture and emerges over the ages from its history, its struggles both military and theological, and its great thoughts. Jewish thought often understands Israel as a people who wrestles with God. Indeed the name Israel may stand for that. It would not be inappropriate to consider the Bible from that perspective, as the story of a people who wrestle with God.

In that context as we read the Bible we may in the company of many others over the ages perceive the hand of God at work in the Bible and the history of the culture which it records. That perception would be the product of interpretation and not historical analysis.

The portrait which the Bible offers us is the picture of a providential God, a God who is concerned for His people, hears and responds to their prayers, and periodically dwells with or is present to them. In the exodus from Egypt God goes before His people in a cloud by day and a pillar of fire by night. After Sinai, God is present to His people in the Ark of the Covenant and then the Temple. Islam and Christianity follow that tradition.

The Christian Bible including the Gospels is written in the context of that tradition. The four gospels, the Acts of the Apostles and the epistles portray a high moment in the presence of God to His people. The Gospel of John as traditionally understood presents a High Christology. The opening passage sets forth his theme in a marvelous hymn which I memorized when I was young. It begins:

"In the beginning was the Word and the Word was with God and the Word was God. He was in the beginning with God; all things were made through him, and without him was not anything made that was made. In him was life, and the life was the life of men. The light shines in the darkness, and the darkness has not overcome it....

"And the Word became flesh and dwelt among us, full of grace and truth; we have beheld his glory, glory as of the only Son from the Father...and from his fullness have we all received; grace upon grace. For the law was given through Moses; grace and truth came through Jesus Christ. No one has ever seen God; the only son, who is in the bosom of the Father; he has made him known."

The disciples of Jesus as portrayed in the Gospels gradually began to perceive His revelation. In the Acts of the Apostles when Peter makes his great speeches he is beginning to approach the High Christology of John's Gospel. Over the remaining centuries of the Roman Empire; the church reflected on and puzzled over the revelation of Jesus. Then in the Nicene Creed the Church convened in Council summarized those reflections as follows:

> "We believe in one God, The Father, the Almighty Maker of heaven and earth, of all that is seen and unseen… We believe in one Lord, Jesus Christ, the only Son of God eternally begotten of the Father, God from God, Light from Light, true God from true God, begotten, not made, one in Being with the Father. Through him all things were made. For us men and for our salvation he came down from heaven by the power of the Holy Spirit he was born of the Virgin Mary and became man."

Traditionally the three synoptic gospels, Matthew, Mark and Luke, do not offer the high Christology we find in John. Rather they recognize Jesus as the Christ, the Messiah. In a recent book,(Ratzinger 2007 at 60), however, the former Cardinal Joseph Ratzinger, now Benedict XVI, a leading theologian, argues that the Synoptic Gospels do offer a high Christology. The Jesus portrayed in those gospels does deeds only proper to God. He forgives sins, for example. In the Sermon on the Mount He offers a major addendum to the commands given by God to Moses on Mount Sinai. The Gospels of Luke and the Acts of the Apostles are usually attributed to the same author. In Acts Peter in one of his great speeches describes Jesus as the Author of life.

Some theologians describe the Synoptic Gospels not merely as narratives of Jesus' life but as exercises designed to lead the reader slowly to recognition of Jesus as the Christ, the Messiah, and the Son of God. That recognition ultimately lead to the great credos of the Nicene Creed.

The Gospel stories and the other writings of the Christian Bible may be perceived or interpreted as the capstone of the Hebrew Bible, the culmination of God's long effort to mold the Hebrew people in preparation for extending their blessings to the Gentiles. Jesus instructs His disciples to preach the Gospel to all nations baptizing them in the name of the Father, the Son, and the Holy Spirit.

The Hebrew Bible portrays God as a providential God who is concerned for and dwells with His people. The Christian Bible brings that story to this logical conclusion: God through His Christ becomes one of us, joins our journey, participates in our sufferings and takes them on as His own.

There is a large objection to the perception that the Christian Bible is the culmination of the story presented by the Hebrew Bible. Over the ages Hebrew Culture wrestled with, insisted upon, fought for and suffered for monotheism, the perception that there was one God and no other beside Him. The Christian doctrine of the Trinity sketched in the Gospels and set forth definitively in the Nicene Creed, one could argue, is not consistent with Hebrew monotheism.

The Nicean Creed, however, explicitly accepts monotheism when it states: "Credo in Unum Deo". That is, "we believe in One God ". Christianity perceives the Trinity as One God. While humans in Biblical thought are made in the image and likeness of God, religious thinkers while acknowledging that always have insisted that God is utterly different than we are. It should not be difficult for modern thought acquainted with psychology, quantum mechanics, and string theory with its multiple dimensions to recognize that God's internal makeup should consist of three personalities or three Persons in close intimate and inseparable relation with each other. As the Nicean Creed puts it the Son is of one substance, or one in Being with the Father. St Patrick used the analogy of a shamrock leaf, one leaf with three parts. That, of course, is an imperfect analogy. In Christian thought the Three Persons reflect, interpenetrate and intimately relate to each other. They are One God., the God who is, Yahweh.

In Christian thought Jesus is not just a continuation of a line of great prophets, perhaps the greatest of the prophets. He is Emmanuel, God with us, the promise of the ages, the logical culmination of the long struggle with God of the Hebrew people, and represents the high point in God's concern for us and His desire to dwell with His people.

Other Objections

Secular thinkers would pose another great objection. Summed up that objection would be: this is a fascinating story, greater than the seven volumes of Harry Potter, but nevertheless only a legendary story.

In reply I would start by noting that the story beginning with the Hebrew Bible and continuing into the Christian has been and is an enormously influential story which has affected the growth of civilization and the conduct of people over the ages and even now at the present. It has roots deep in the history of the Hebrew culture beginning perhaps as early as 1500 B.C. but certainly was a great influence by the reign of King David.

God promised Abraham that his descendents would be more numerous than the stars of the sky and promised the Hebrew people that their blessings would extend to the Gentiles. Taking due note of John the Baptizer's statement that God can raise up descendents to Abraham from these rocks, that is indeed what has happened. At the time of King David about 900 B.C. only Israel worshipped one God. Now most of the ancient pagan religions have vanished. Three great religions worship one God and honor Abraham representing billions of people, about half the world. Our culture is permeated with moral values developed from ancient Hebrew thought and Christian revelation.

The animal sacrifices of the Hebrew religion and similar sacrifices of the surrounding pagan world have largely vanished. Human sacrifice, a recurring feature of the pagan world which the Hebrew prophets declaimed against also has largely disappeared. The blessings of Abraham indeed have been extended to the Gentile world.

On a minor note many secular thinkers and some who are religious would have difficulty with the miracles found throughout the Bible but particularly in the Gospels. Miracles appear to them to be irrational, as unreasonable interferences with the laws of science and of nature. One should note that we, myself and those reading this, were not present at the time of those miracles and therefore cannot testify to them. In my recognition of God's presence I do not rely on the reports of those miracles to support my perception of God. However, I do not find the notion of miracles shocking. The power of God is enormous. I find no reason why He should not occasionally interfere in nature. In the modern world of science where chance and even chaos are influential notions, where random mutation is an important aspect of evolution, where as the Heisenberg Uncertainty Principle explains we cannot predict the location of an electron and measure its speed at the same time, there is ample room for intervention by a Providential God. Along with many other religious persons I recognize the regular intervention by God in my own life as I examine my ongoing experience.

Human Suffering and the Suffering of Christ

An important objection to a Providential God is the regular presence in our world of extensive human suffering. In commenting on that problem one should note first as explained above that we live in a necessarily imperfect world.

Only God is perfect. In Christian theology God generates a Second Person, the Word of God, the Son, within and from His Own Being. That Person intimately related to the Father mirrors the Father exactly.

If God out of overflowing love wants to create someone or something other than Himself, that person and that world necessarily must be imperfect. Only God is perfect. The question then becomes what kind of world will be created with what degree of imperfection. There is no reason to believe that our world is not the best choice among a number of alternatives. Certainly most of the worlds imagined in science fiction all are less desirable, perhaps considerably less, than the world as we know it.

God as described earlier is this essay has chosen to create an evolutionary world. Beginning with the Big Bang the universe slowly develops over time. I perceive it as a great engineering feat involving the creation and use of a number of great systems. Our earth also slowly develops over time. Again I perceive the creation of the earth as a great work of engineering. A number of great systems combine to produce the earth as we know it. The genetic system is one of those and life evolves in the circumstances presented by the interactions of these great systems.

Evolving life necessarily changes and develops, faces and overcomes challenges. As we know the world, that necessarily presents the possibility of suffering and struggle, success and failure. As argued earlier in this essay an evolutionary world also allows a place for free will, for human freedom, for co-creation of our world by human beings, for providential intervention by God, for development, change, repentance and reform. An evolutionary world offers the possibility of second chances.

In the world as we know it human suffering is inevitable. The presence of human suffering is a serious situation not to be shrugged off. Around the turn of the nineteenth and twentieth century my grandmother's and grandfather's family was growing up in Jersey City, New Jersey. At that time a diphtheria epidemic struck. Within a short period of time my grandmother and grandfather lost five small children. I am the descendant of their second family. That is only a small example of the great suffering in the world. Imagine the destruction of New Orleans, the devastation left by earthquakes and hurricanes and then the product of human evil, the Holocaust, the atomic destruction of Hiroshima

When we move from the inevitability of imperfection in the physical world to moral contemplation of the human circumstances an enormous challenge is presented. Confronted with the inevitability of imperfection and suffering should God have chosen not to create? My answer is that He should have chosen to create; to pursue the goodness of creation in the presence of enormous problems including the inevitability of extensive traumatic human suffering.

Nevertheless, a God who loves must necessarily out of His love, confront and address that inevitable imperfection, the struggles of evolution and growth and of human success and failure in co-creation of the world. God, as One who loves must be troubled enormously by the traumas of human suffering.

One response recorded in the Hebrew and Christian Bibles is periodic providential intervention in the human struggle. Many religious persons recognize the regular intervention of God in their lives. I thank God each day for his constant care and protection.

The great response presented in the Christian Bible, in the Gospels, the Acts of the Apostles and the epistles is that God became one of us, joined in our journey, in our co-creation, took on our imperfection and our suffering as His own. As the poems point out this is a God to love, a God who understands and participates, a God to whom His suffering creatures can cry out as one who loves, suffers with us and understands.

The Sacrifice of Christ

A significant portion of human suffering is due to natural events, to disease, sickness, hurricanes, earthquakes, floods and the like. Another significant portion, however, is caused by the evil actions of other human beings, from economic exploitation to the deliberate infliction of suffering sometimes on the vast scale of the Holocaust. Evil, extensive evil, has been a part of human life as far back in history as we can go. From cannibalism among early modern humans to human sacrifice, to the mass crucifixions in the Mediterranean world particularly by Alexander the Great and the Roman Empire, to the Holocaust, to the atomic bombing of Japan, to suicide bombings and gang murder, evil inflicted by human beings is constantly present in our world. Sometimes we seem to be immersed in and overcome by evil. God's response to suffering, then, should include His response to evil among human beings.

Evil, as traditionally understood, is present in part because human beings have free will. Free will is one of our precious possessions. It is the foundation of human freedom. It allows us to freely choose love, which may not be love unless freely chosen. It also allows us to choose evil. And many of us have. As a result evil has become part of human culture. Encountering and wrestling with evil is a part of human growth and development in this world as we find it. In some circumstances for example, the Nazism of the mid-twentieth century, the evil a developing young person encounters is pervasive. In parts of the Roman Empire one also might perceive pervasive evil.

One response recorded in the Gospels is forgiveness. God forgives our sins. Jesus forgives the sins of those He encounters. He instructs us to forgive each other. Forgiveness allows us to start again both individually and together. In our human circumstances it appears necessary to love. Modern thought would find forgiveness important in family life, to peace in society, to healing breeches caused by war and revolution, for example, in post World War Europe and in Ireland.

A traditional understanding of Christianity is that the sacrifice of Christ, His death on the Cross, atones to the Father for the sins of humanity, redeems us from our sins both individually and collectively and allows us to be saved by accepting Christ as our Savior.

Some critics of Christianity would find this understanding barbaric. How can God the Father be a loving God if He demands the bloody sacrifice of His Son as the price for the salvation of humankind? Pope Benedict XVI, the former Joseph Ratzinger, in a book, Introduction to Christianity, published earlier in his career as a theologian, and republished on his ascent to the papacy, agrees. He attributes this theory which he calls legalistic to Bishop Anselm of Canterbury (ca. 1033-1109) and then argues that this "legal system erected by Anselm distorts the perspective and with its rigid logic can make the image of God appear in a sinister light." He follows this critique of Anselm with a very important passage describing insights relevant both to evolution and to the incarnation, to God becoming one of us.

I want to request your patient tolerance while I quote this passage in full:

> "The Rubricon of becoming man, of "hominzation' was first crossed by the step from animal to *logos*, from mere life to mind. Man came into existence out of the 'clay' at the moment when a creature was no longer merely 'there' but over and above just being there and filling his needs, was aware of the whole. But this step, through which *logos*, understanding, mind, first came into this world, is only completed when the *Logos* itself, the whole creative meaning, and man merge into each other. Man's full "hominzation" presupposes God's becoming man; only by this event is the

Rubricon dividing the '*anima*' from the 'logical' finally crossed for ever and the highest possible development accorded to the process that began when a creature of dust and earth looked out beyond itself and its environment and was able to address God as "You". It is openness to the whole, to the infinite, that makes man complete. Man is man by reaching out infinitely beyond himself, and he is consequently more of a man the less enclosed he is in himself, the less 'limited' he is. For-let me repeat—that man is most fully man, indeed *the* true man, who is most unlimited, who not only has contact with the infinite-the infinite Being—but is one with him: Jesus Christ. In him 'hominzation' has truly reached its goal." (Ratzinger 1969, 2004 at 231)

In this passage the former Cardinal Ratzinger puts the Incarnation, God becoming man in the person of Jesus, the Christ, in the context of evolution. God, according to Ratzinger, means to join man in his evolution, his co-creation of the world, in his journey toward the infinite. God means to relate to man and to bring man into relation with God. And He means to do this in the context of this evolutionary world which He has created.

When God encounters a human, evolutionary world in which evil is seriously present (probably because freewill has run amok) He must take that world as it is and as a responsible person take on that evil and seek to transform it.

An objection arises here. Shouldn't an all powerful God confronted with evil simply wave His magic wand and transform that world totally eliminating the evil? This has been a troublesome problem for many since the crucifixion. An answer would be that God created an evolutionary world in which man has free will and does not mean to change that but to transform it gradually from within.

In that context I propose a theory of the sacrifice of Christ. The presentation of that theory should be in several steps:

A. Throughout the Hebrew Bible, God is critical of animal sacrifice. I do not need the blood of goats and bulls, He explains. If I were hungry, He adds, I would not tell you. God seeks mercy and not sacrifice. That last phrase is repeated several times in the Gospels.

B. God nevertheless allows the animal sacrifices in the Jewish Temple. During the Exodus from Egypt the feast of Passover is established. An important feature of that feast is the eating of the Passover Lamb. At the time of Jesus the family's Passover Lamb was sacrificed in the Temple before being returned to the family for the feast.

C. In the evolutionary context of religion, of God wrestling with a people, transforming and molding them, he should develop and complete their understanding of sacrifice, including the sacrifice of the Pascal lamb.

D. An important transformation of the notion of sacrifice is found in the writings of the Hebrew prophets and repeated several times in the Gospels. The prophet says—Holocausts and sin offerings you would not accept, so I say here I am. I come to do your will. Send me. We regularly speak of heroic actions, including those in war, as sacrifices. We talk of sacrificing one's life for one's country or for the sake of others. We consider such acts admirable and do not compare them to the human sacrifices of the pagan religions.

E. In the Hebrew Bible God seriously opposes human sacrifice. There is a peculiar part of the story of Abraham. God directs Abraham to sacrifice his son Isaac. At the moment of sacrifice God stops Abraham who then sees a ram caught in the bushes and as a substitute sacrifices that. This story has become the subject of much theological reflection both in the Jewish and Christian religions. I would offer an unsophisticated guess that it originally was written as a parable in opposition to human sacrifice. Nevertheless over time it became an important symbol. John the Baptizer refers to Jesus as the Lamb of God, the substitute sacrifice akin to the ram found by Abraham in the bushes.

F. I would offer a further interpretation of that concept of substitute sacrifice. The death of Jesus the Christ on the Cross is not a human sacrifice in any traditional sense of the word. God opposes human sacrifice and does not accept sacrifices of that form. He even opposes animal sacrifice although He was willing to tolerate and accept them as a temporary expedient in the course of evolution. Rather the sacrifice of

Christ is in a different category, in the same category as heroic sacrifices in war, or of a fireman's life as he tries to save people from a burning house.

G. In support of that last point I would note that Christ's death on the cross has no immediate ritual resemblance to the Temple sacrifices or to the human sacrifices of the pagan religions. He is executed by Roman soldiers in a manner used regularly to oppress subordinate peoples and suppress their rebels. Christ's death is akin to the deaths of many Irish rebels at the hands of the British.

H. Here I am, says the prophet, I come to do your will. Jesus comes to do the Father's will, that is, to fully identify with human beings, to become one of us, to share our journey and our sufferings, to identify with us even in death. He means to challenge the evils of this world, to cure the sick for example, to criticize hypocrites and self-serving public and religious officials. Ultimately He challenges the establishment of His day including the Roman oppressors and willingly suffers the consequences of that. That challenge is symbolized by His triumphant entry into Jerusalem which we celebrate on Palm Sunday. Jesus as the Word of God, the Messiah, came to do His Father's will, to identify with us, our struggles and sufferings. That is His heroic sacrifice, akin to the sacrifice of a soldier in war or a fireman in a burning building.

I. In the Christian Bible the death of Christ on the Cross is followed by His resurrection. He has faced and conquered death. It also is followed by the transformation of His apostles and disciples who shortly after (apparently within a few months) begin to preach in His name, to continue His challenge to the existing establishment, to make converts all over Judea and Samaria. See the Acts of the Apostles. Beyond that with frequent interventions from the Holy Spirit, they follow Jesus' instructions, to preach the Gospel to the ends of the earth, baptizing them in the name of the Father, the Son, and the Holy Spirit. Within 300 years of Jesus' death the Roman Empire officially becomes Christian. The blessings of Abraham are being extended to the Gentiles.

J. The sacrifice of Jesus the Christ is the act of a leader who will not ask His followers to do anything He is not prepared to do. The transformation of the Roman Empire begins with Jesus' triumphant entry

217

into Jerusalem on Palm Sunday, continues through His crucifixion and resurrection and on through the ages. The Roman Empire was oppressing His people. He leads His followers to the Conquest of the Roman Empire not by force or war but by love and by the willingness to suffer for their beliefs. Jesus the Christ has come to do His Father's will and to extend the blessings of Abraham to the Gentiles. That is the sacrifice of the Christ, to do the Father's will even at the cost of his life. Note that He does this in a manner consistent with the cultural evolution of human beings, their co-creation and their free will. He does not wave a magic wand. Those who wish He did have always refused to recognize Jesus as the Christ.

K. Please note the theory or explanation just sketched of the sacrifice of Jesus the Christ while offering an alternative to the thought of Anselm of Canterbury is nevertheless consistent with traditional Christian thought. On the night before He died Jesus ate the Passover Supper with His disciples thereby establishing a ritual framework for His sacrifice on the cross. Jesus is the Passover lamb, the Lamb of God. He not only is a substitute sacrifice for humans and animals He transforms the notion of sacrifice. One offers oneself to God by doing God's will, by serving others (see the washing of the feet), by leading the followers of God and by preaching His word even in the face of death. Jesus is the first in a long line of Christian martyrs. The early Christians including St. Paul in his letter to the Romans and the author of the letter to the Hebrews rapidly put a theological framework on the sacrifice of Christ which became the center of Christian belief and ritual. The theory just offered is not meant to replace that theological framework. It simply analyzes the nature of Jesus' sacrifice.

L. The sacrifice of Jesus the Christ as so understood can satisfy God's anger with humankind. Here is a human person who also is God, prepared to do God's will, to transform humanity, to die in the effort, but to continue that labor over the ages. If one is seriously attached to the theory of Anselm of Canturbury, it still works only slightly transformed. Here is a human who also is God, who can offer infinite satisfaction to the Father for the transgressions of humankind, who offers His life in the effort to transform and convert the world. The nature of the sacrifice is transformed, but the heroic sacrifice remains and should be more satisfying yet to a loving Father.

M. Another understanding could rest on the inspiration of an additional episode from the story of Abraham. God visits Abraham on His way to Sodom and Gommorah. In the course of discussion Abraham begins to bargain with God. You would not destroy those cities, he says, if you could find 50 just men there. Abraham ultimately bargains God down to 10 just men. In accordance with the theory sketched above, Jesus the Christ is one just man prepared to die in order to do the Father's will, to redirect the cultural evolution of the world, to start its transformation and to generate generations of followers some of whom also could pass on occasion for just men and women.

Jesus is prepared to lead the transformation of the world through the leaven of his teaching, the drama of his confrontation with Rome and the quisling government of Jerusalem, his challenge to death and his overcoming of it through his Resurrection. The reconciliation of God to the world is accomplished by the commencement of the world's transformation. Jesus' offering to the Father is his provision of the leaven which will gradually permeate the world until all is leavened. "Here I am, Lord," He says, "I come to do your will."

Altogether, I prefer Cardinal Ratzinger's theory that God through His Christ is for us. Christ identifies with us fully, with our suffering and death, joins us in our journey and transforms that journey. Christ is God for us and with us. He transforms human life and human death. That is the will of the Father. The sacrifice of Christ is to do the Father's will. The poems reflect that understanding. Cardinal Ratzinger continues to insist on the Christian transformation of the Passover ritual. Jesus is the Lamb of God. I would comment as above that Jesus is not only the substitute sacrifice, He transforms the notion of sacrifice. He has come to do the Father's will even in the face of death. That is His sacrificial offering. He comes to fully identify with us, with our suffering and death, and to lead us in our continuing transformation of the world even at the cost of considerable sacrifice, even at the cost of encountering death. He comes to defy death and to transform our understanding of death. That is the Father's will. The sacrifice of Jesus is to do the Father's will. Following

Jesus, our sacrifice is to continue to do the Father's will, to take up our crosses and follow Jesus in the continuing transformation of the world.

It may be helpful to restate what has just been said in more traditional terms which also make sense and are agreeable to me. In this restatement it is important to note that Jesus' whole life is a sacrifice as described above. During the closing episode of his life on earth there is a clear linkage between the Passover Supper, His Last Supper, the Crucifixion, His Resurrection from the dead, and His sending of the Holy Spirit. All are part of His effort to do the Father's will, to restart our cultural evolution and transform the world. Each of these events is closely connected with the others.

Once God made a covenant with Abraham. Following God's promises to him, Abraham asks—how am I to know that I will have this. The Biblical scholars tell us this is not an arrogant untrusting question but simply a normal request to establish a formal covenant which God complies with by passing in fire through Abraham's offerings.

The three overwhelming great events of Holy Week, the establishment of the Eucharist at the Passover meal on Holy Thursday, Christ's death on the Cross on Good Friday and His resurrection from the dead on Easter Sunday together may interpreted, as is traditional, as a similar establishment of a formal covenant. This as Christ explains when establishing the Eucharist is the "New Covenant in My Blood", the transforming example and symbol of God's presence with us in our sufferings, of His challenge to human oppression and tyranny, of His encounter with and overcoming of death not only for Himself but for us, and His willing to be with us in our sufferings and stumbling efforts to do God's will and establish His kingdom of love.

By His death on the Cross Jesus completes the task begun by His incarnation and birth. God though the Second Person of the Trinity has completely identified Himself with humanity, with us, with our lives, our difficulties, our sufferings. Having created a developing, changing, and necessarily imperfect world, God like an exemplary great leader undertakes to lead us through life, to do and suffer those things which He has asked us, His people, to go through. On the Cross He completes His acceptance of and identification with the suffering of the world, suffering made worse by our sins and constant recourse to tyranny and violence.

In the Eucharist, Jesus transforms the bread and wine into His body and blood. At the Passover meal, He eats the "bread of affliction which our fathers ate in the desert". It is this unleavened bread which He transforms into His body and offers to His disciples telling them "Take this all of you and eat it. This is My Body which will be given up for you." This, then, is the Bread of Heaven which is the life of the world, the daily bread of the Our Father, the Life of God which He shares with us and without which we cannot have eternal life. The Eucharist also symbolizes [a real example as well as a symbol] that God can transform anything, the bread of affliction, you and I, and share His Life with us.

In the Old Testament God makes clear that He does not want sacrifice in the traditional sense. You want mercy and not sacrifice, says the prophet. Burnt offerings you would not accept. So I said: "Here I am, send me." The prophet perceives his willingness to offer himself for God's work as the substitute for burnt offerings.

Just so with Jesus. His death on the Cross is not a sacrifice in the traditional sense of burnt offerings in the Temple or even Aztec human sacrifice. Rather it is the culmination of God's work of identifying Himself with us and our sufferings in this imperfect world made more imperfect by our sin and violence. It is the example to His followers of how to confront evil in the world, and the commencement of that confrontation. At the same time it is a confrontation with and the overcoming of death and a great sign which will move and convert millions throughout the ages. Jesus like the Old Testament prophet says "Send Me" to perform this great work and provide this great sign of God's covenant, of His acceptance of us and His identification with us and our difficulties and suffering.

Of all the difficulties of this imperfect world one of the most troublesome to God must be death. Only God has eternal life; everything and everyone else must come to an end. We can live forever only if God shares His Life with us. The full sign of the new covenant is present when God raises Jesus from the dead, a confirmation and sign of the fulfillment of Jesus' promise to raise all of us from the dead.

Like Jesus our undertaking in this new covenant, the sacrifice of our life, is to accept this covenant by offering our lives for the work of God. As Jesus changes the bread of affliction into His Body, He can transform us as following in His footsteps we do God's work.

In the final week of His Life Jesus enters Jerusalem to lead His people, to complete His life of good works by challenging an oppressive regime of quislings backed by a tyrannical occupying power. He knows the highly likely result but completes God's work with this challenge, a replication of God's challenge through Moses to the Pharaoh of Egypt and the predecessor to innumerable challenges to worldly tyranny and oppression. At the same moment Jesus challenges death, the greatest imperfection in this imperfect world and on Easter Sunday overcomes it, a great sign of God's covenant with us as we do his work confronting the evils of our world, and are transformed by God as we begin to share His life.

From God's perspective, as my son Sam suggests, His Absolute Love for us humans deserves an absolute love in return which we alone cannot accomplish. In the Trinity's relation of love, however, God can return absolute love to God by becoming man and doing God's will and work. By God becoming man, man is capable of returning absolute love. As we are transformed by sharing God's Life we can share in that return of absolute love. Jesus at His Baptism by John the Baptist, as traditionally understood, identifies with sinners. He takes our sins with Him to the cross and by the return of Absolute Love wipes out our sins.

Fit

One of the poems exclaims: This is a God to love. The Christian Story emerging from 1,000 years or more of a great culture described in the Hebrew Bible continues and dramatically emphasizes a theme of Hebrew history that God is a Providential God concerned for us and prepared to dwell with us in the tent, the Ark of the Covenant, and the Temple. In the Christian Bible this God joins our journey, becomes one of us and dies for us. His followers then guided by His leadership and accompanied by His power bring the blessings of Abraham to the gentiles and act as a leaven in our cultural evolution. This is a God to love.

This story beginning with Abraham and continuing to the present offers a powerful answer to the human search for meaning in our universe, our world. It is consistent with an evolutionary understanding of our earth and our culture. Rather than waving a magic wand, God joins our struggles and provides a leaven for our cultural evolution. One can recognize God's presence in our world only if one is not looking for a magic wand.

This story supports our highest ideals. When Jesus is asked what one must do to attain everlasting life, His first reply is—keep the commandments. The commandments secure order and peace in society and justice between ourselves and our fellow humans. His ultimate commands to love our neighbors as ourselves and to love one another as He has loved us establish perhaps for the first time the highest goals of human activity which have inspired us ever since.

When told to love his neighbor as himself one interlocutor then asks: and who is my neighbor Lord. Jesus replies with the story of the Good Samaritan who rescues a man wounded by robbers and lying by the side of the road. At the end of the story Jesus asks: who proved himself neighbor to the man who fell among robbers. The reply is—the one who came to his aid. Jesus then adds—go and do likewise.

This story exemplifies concrete love as distinguished from abstract sentiments as indeed does Jesus' life and presence in this world as the Son of God. God's presence with us and this story have inspired concrete social action and service to others ever since from the early Christians to the present.

The story of the Christ fits with the evolutionary nature of our developing culture, acting as a leaven. That story fits with and inspires our highest ideals. It also fits well with a world of suffering and sin. God joins our journey and suffers with us. In this story from Abraham to the present, in this story of God with us, we can perceive the presence of God in the life and evolutionary development of humans as we find ourselves on this planet.

Earlier in this essay we discussed the presence of God in the history and scientific laws of the universe from the Big Bang through three generations of stars to the structuring of our earth. We have discussed evolution and the possibility of perceiving God in the events which led to the Age of Mammals and their evolution. In the story from Abraham to the present, the story of God with us, we find God present in the history of humans, in their cultural evolution, in their suffering and in their growth, development, ideals, and achievements.

Finding God in all these ways, and we should add in the constant presence of beauty, exemplifies the virtue of fit. The perception of God in multiple aspects of the universe as we know it supports and checks out the many particular ways in which we discern God's presence.

One of the poems, Discerning God, finds it particularly hard to discern God in the bloody history of our cultural evolution. The story of the Christ who joins our journey and shares our suffering, continuing the story of a culture which found God continually and regularly present, makes discerning the presence of God in our bloody history possible. When we recognize how that story fits our ideals and circumstances the perception of God's presence becomes powerful. As the next to final poem asserts this story, the story of the Christ, is the jigsaw piece which fits the puzzle. It has the virtue of fit.

The perception of a providential God who is regularly present to us, who joins our journey and shares our suffering also fits the on-going experience of many religious persons and some who once were not religious. Over the ages and even in the present many persons have and will testify to their experience of the presence and providence of God. That testimony supports the perception of fit. Looking back over one's life one often perceives when God has aided, rescued or influenced us. I too add my testimony, I know the times and places; I know when God has rescued me.

An objection to this perception which often is offered may be stated as follows: Christianity has not changed our world; evil, sometimes enormous evil, continues to trouble us; Christianity simply offers us the proverbial pie in the sky. In reply the following points among others should be made.

A. At the time of Christ, the Roman Empire, however beneficial to

224

world peace at the time was pervasively oppressive to non-Romans and in places was pervasively evil. Only Judea worshipped one God. Pagan religions sometimes with strange rites were the norm. The notion of human rights and respect for the dignity of each and every person had not been thought of except perhaps in Israel under the concept of justice or for Roman citizens.

B. While ancient religions still are important in some parts of the world, generally our model of religion today at least in the West and indeed more generally is monotheism.

C. By and large animal sacrifice and more importantly human sacrifice are obsolete.

D. We have a growing concern for human rights and the dignity of each person. While the ideology of human rights has a complex history and was distinctly jump started during the Enlightenment, its foundation may be found in the Hebrew concept of justice and in the teachings of Jesus such as his direction to love your neighbor as yourself and love one another as "I" have loved you.

E. Much of the Roman world was uneducated. Beginning with the great monasteries and then continuing with the first universities, Oxford, Paris, Bologna, the Christian Church laid the foundations for modern education.

F. Concern for the poor is a modern ideal. That ideal is promoted in the Hebrew Bible and in Jewish practice and heavily emphasized in the Gospels. Christ identifies with the poorest-what you do to the least of my brethren, you do unto Me, He explains. Regard for the poor with some exception for the Roman mob was not high on the Roman Empire's agenda.

G. God promised that the blessings of Abraham would be extended to the Gentiles. Before the time of Christ only modest progress had been made on that agenda. Now Christianity has spread to much of the world. That extension of the ideals and monotheism of Israel began with the Roman Empire which was converted non-violently within 300 years of the death of Christ.

H. God in His presence to the Hebrew people and Jesus during this life and thereafter did not wave a magic wand. Rather God proceeded slowly both in Hebrew history and in the Christian world. Jesus declared that His teachings would act as a leaven in society's culture until all is leavened. In other words God in Hebrew history and since Jesus has worked to slowly mold human cultural evolution. We can observe today the advance in human civilization traceable to Jesus the Christ and to the preceding Hebrew culture. Some of those advances were just listed. Perhaps the most important of these is the ideal of love of neighbor and love of God which is influential today but which was not important in the Roman Empire.

A second important objection is that it would have been better for the peace of the world and the future of religion for God to remain content with a general and mystical monotheism. By coming to one people (Israel) and then converting one culture, primarily the Western, God laid the basis for future discord, discrimination, oppression and war.

In reply note that the teachings of Jesus are in opposition to discord, discrimination, oppression and war. God created an evolutionary world and Jesus' teachings operate in that context as a leaven, a leaven that appears still to be working.

If God had been content to be a mystical monotheist God and not a God who joined His people's journey and participated in their sufferings He would not so clearly be a God to serve and a God who loves. The great Christian ideal of love would be absent from our world or would appear only in an anemic form. Suffering people would not be able to cry out to a God who suffered and understands.

In conclusion we have just discussed the virtue or quality of fit. We have been applying a method of checking out used in law, philosophy and other fields to determine how well an insight or theory fits with the relevant structures or circumstances. For example, does our interpretation of the First Amendment's protection of freedom of speech fit with our understanding of the entire Constitution? Does an interpretation of a painting fit with what we can observe about the structure of the painting and what we know of the artist's work?

Compare the task of doing a jigsaw puzzle. When finding the right place in a puzzle for a particular piece we have an "insight", a bright idea, that it's shape fits at a certain point in the configuration of the puzzle. In the case of a jigsaw puzzle we can instantly verify that fit and if it fails try another piece. When we are dealing with larger structures over which we do not have as great control, fit nevertheless may be an appropriate checking out of an insight, here the recognition of a Providential God in the beauty and scientific laws of the universe, in the systems that built our earth, in the evolution of life, animal and human, and in our cultural evolution. The converging perceptions of God's presence in each of these aspects of our world, the world we are sorting out, support our perception of fit. Fit also is present as discussed above in particular aspects of the world: The perceived presence of God, a God who joins our journey, restarts our cultural evolution and shares our sufferings fits with the tragedies and triumphs of human life.

Faith, Reason and Recognition

Recognition is related to insight and fit. One could understand it as a form of insight. An example of recognition is when we perceive that one of the persons we associate with is a friend or a good person. We also may have moments in which we recognize others as human beings capable of friendship, suffering, desire for goodness, going through struggles, having feelings and inadequacies just like ourselves. That is an insight basic to ethical commitment, to respect and concern for others. An advantage of modern television and world wide reporting is that the process of recognition can allow us to understand persons across the world as human beings like ourselves and allow us to develop ethical commitments across the boundaries of nations, geography and culture.

Recognition of others as persons occurs in the context of human experience, of on-going relations with others. In that context a number of factors, experiences, words, actions merge together to produce an insight which can be checked out against our range of experiences and future experience.

The coming together of factors, this convergence of probabilities which establishes a reasonable foundation for recognition can be illustrated by an example not as closely related to persons and ethical commitment. Imagine a person who had visited the city of London, toured it, seen it and experienced it. A few years later at nine o'clock in the morning that person is asked in the course of conversation whether the city of London now exists. Given modern communications and the mass media it is reasonable to conclude with strong certainty that London existed a half hour ago at eight thirty. The certainty that London exists at this very moment is a little bit less. Those degrees of certainty are the result of a convergence of probabilities. In the course of our everyday lives we make a number of decisions on the basis of such a convergence of probabilities. Skill at making reasonable decisions on the basis of such insights is important to survival and successful living.

An argument in this essay is that we can use our skill at recognition to perceive an intelligent and beneficent person at work in the development of the universe from the Big Bang to the present, in the pervasive presence of scientific law throughout that development, in the systems that structured our earth where scientific laws again were pervasively present, in the evolution of life, in the constant and gratuitous presence of beauty throughout and finally in human cultural evolution and the evidence of the intervention of a providential God found in the Hebrew and Christian Bibles and the subsequent history of religion.

That perception inevitably will encounter problems because of the multiple cultural and religious horizons in our world. In the academy with its many disciplines, methodologies and departments that perception again will be disputed. Horizons both create and restrict our vision. If you leave college and go to law school thereby acquiring new horizons you will understand much that you did not know about before but you also will lose interest in and cease to understand or be interested in other disciplines which could have affected you. Horizons both allow and block vision. Scientists, mathematicians and others may have difficulty understanding the notion of recognition. We already have insisted that the perception of God in the development of the universe and the evolution of life is not science. Rather that perception goes beyond science.

Nevertheless some will object that the recognition of God goes well beyond the foundations for recognition in human experience. It inappropriately applies our understanding of human beings to realms far beyond that human experience. Theologians and others call that anthropomorphism. Religious thinkers while recognizing God nevertheless often carefully guard their thought against anthropomorphism. It should be noted that there are no crude anthropomorphic concepts offered in this essay or in the poetry. Any accusation of anthropomorphism would have to rest on the application of the process of recognition derived from human experience to an interpretation of the universe and the perception there of a higher being.

Our understanding of intellectual method nevertheless is always derived from our human experience. Many of us put artificial restrictions on our application of method. Arguably those who refuse to apply our human understanding to the perception of a higher intelligence at work in the universe are engaged in such artificial restriction.

One should add that the foundations for the perception of an intelligent and beneficent person at work in our universe are there and will not go away. Despite intelligent objections that perception cannot be fundamentally refuted. Therefore the perception of the presence of God raised on those foundations will continue to puzzle, annoy, or amaze humans over the ages.

The argument in this essay and in the poetry is that it is reasonable to perceive the presence of God. I along with many others find that perception compelling.

Faith

Recognition or similar language often appears in discussions of faith. The great religious song, "Amazing Grace", contains the line "I once was blind but now I see". The Gospels are full of references to blindness and sight, to the inability to understand or to the light which leads us to understanding. Recognition perhaps through the crossing of horizons, through long experience, or a sudden insight is an important prelude to faith.

Recognition nevertheless is not Faith. Faith is a gift from God and often develops in mysterious ways. Often recognition precedes faith but perhaps not always. Faith for example, and perhaps recognition can rest on cultural familiarity. Those brought up in a faith may accept that faith and may be able to understand and perceive because of their familiarity with that horizon. When recognition precedes faith or for those who already believe when recognition precedes deeper faith, that recognition may occur in many different circumstances, in different sizes and shapes, as I sometimes say.

My own development as a believer had many twists and turns and changes over a lifetime. The more mature presentation in this essay and in the poetry is the product of a long life, much experience, and voracious reading. It is far beyond the primitive beginning of my faith. This book is designed to be helpful to those seeking faith and to believers seeking further understanding. It should not be misunderstood as laying down a prescribed way or necessary formula for faith. Faith is a gift from God and comes to us in mysterious ways.

Recognizing that Faith is a gift from God and arises in mysterious ways, some reflection on the meaning of faith may nevertheless be helpful.

The word, belief, has many meanings. One meaning, perhaps derived from faith but not now related to it defines belief as justified opinion. For example, one may say I believe that Peter Smith is the best candidate for President. That may be a wise statement based on experience and analysis but that is not what we mean by religious faith. Like recognition, however, justifiable opinion may be a prelude to religious faith.

Another use of the word belief is closer to what we mean by religious faith. John Jones is about to run a race or take an examination. His mother says, "Johnny I have confidence in you, I know you will do well. I have faith in you. I believe in you." Belief in this sense, is a statement of confidence, trust and commitment.

The former Cardinal Ratzinger, an important theologian who became Pope, in his book, Introduction to Christianity, describes faith as taking a stand. In his view, and mine, Christian belief represents and is based on a rational understanding of the universe. It is an understanding that accepts reason, science and scientific laws and perceives God as the rational support for a rational universe. When one takes a stand for God, one takes a stand in support of understanding, in support of the foundations for a rational understanding of the universe. One also takes a stand which supports our highest ideals and which enables us to embrace our neighbors with love and forgiveness. Christianity presents us with a God who loves us, with a God whom we can love. As the poem explains: "This is a God to love". Embracing Christianity puts love and not tears at the heart of our universe.

When one takes a stand one decides. A decision may be based on knowledge, recognition, insight, or justifiable opinion but the decision as decision is not any one of those. It is a choice, here a choice to believe, to commit oneself to God, to trust in Him or, to use traditional language, to accept Jesus as my personal Savior. That decision and the ability to make it and persist in it is a gift of God. It represents and establishes an interpersonal relationship with God. And to quote the song again: "How wonderful did that grace appear, the hour I first believed."

An inadequate parallel but perhaps a helpful comparison is the decision to marry another person. That decision is a commitment, an expression of trust and faith. It may be based on long acquaintance, on knowledge of the other person, on recognition of him or her as good. Nevertheless, the decision to marry goes beyond those preludes. It is a decision and a commitment. The slang phrase, "So you decided to take the plunge", may be an appropriate description. Writers about religion often refer in a parallel fashion to "the leap of faith". At some point you must decide to take a stand.

In the Hebrew Bible, the prophet Elijah on a mountain top catches a glimpse of God. My recommendation, based in part on my own experience, is that if you catch a glimpse of God, a moment of recognition, you should seize upon that experience and pursue it until you have reached a decision to believe.

That decision, again, is a gift of God and may come early or late in mysterious circumstances perhaps in confusion, perhaps in great clarity. As the poem remarks recognition is a prelude to faith; the early disciples inquired of Jesus, "Rabbi, where do you live," and He replied, "Come and see".

"Come and see". Prayer is a vital method for making the acquaintance of God. Pray for faith. Pray that God gives you the recognition that could serve as a prelude to faith. Pray regularly, humbly and with great desire. Actually go to Church and pray. Attend religious services. Begin to act as if you believed.

In the Gospel Jesus urges us to pray with persistence and adds: ask and you shall receive, knock and it shall be opened to you. At the same time, read and inquire. Read the Gospels. Read them prayerfully. Read a good foundations book. The best one I have found is Joseph Ratzinger, an Introduction to Christianity.(Ratzinger 1969, 2004). A helpful book is the Four Witnesses.(Griffin-Jones 2000). For a more oblique approach read some of the many excellent books by Henri Nouwen or by Thomas Merton whose books I do not like as well as Nouwen's.

Begin to act as a follower of Jesus. That is part of coming and seeing where he lives. In the Gospels Jesus identifies with the poor. What you do to one of these, the least of my brethren you do unto Me, He explains. Work in a soup kitchen. Help Habitat for Humanity. Work with Literacy Volunteers. Somehow or other make personal contact with the poor and serve them. Giving to the poor is good. Personal service is better. And then start the process referred to in the next part as sorting out the churches. You may, of course, already have a good choice between the churches.

One note of caution. If you are a young person in late High School or early College you are a person for whom this book is written. If you have gotten this far in this essay you probably have strong intelligence and persistence. If you are one of my grandchildren I am proud of you. From my own experience, however, you may be excessively proud of your own intelligence. That pride and high intelligence has its moments but may be a stumbling block. God favors the humble rather than the arrogant. Approach God humbly, as a seeker and not with arrogance.

Sorting out the Churches

To review: I find the grounds for perceiving a providential God in the origins and development of our universe, in the structures of our earth, in human evolution, in the religions descended from Abraham and their history and in human experience, persuasive. When confronted with Christianity and its understanding of God as one who loves and who loves us, I find that understanding as it emerges from thousands of years of history not only persuasive but compelling. Again it is necessary to perceive our world in the process of evolution and Christianity as a leaven in our cultural evolution, to perceive in modern times the providential and loving work of God.

Having made a choice in favor of Christianity on these or similar grounds, one can recognize respectfully that he or she has set aside not only the pagan religions and the vague and mystical religions, however appealing, but also our religious ancestor, Judaism, and our close cousin, Islam. Those last two along with Christianity are religions descended from Abraham and share with Christianity the perception of a God who is with us. Christianity, however, carries that perception, that history, to the additional step of recognizing that God through His Christ has joined our journey and shared our sufferings. This is a God to love. That perception and recognition makes Christianity a compelling choice. That perception then becomes a foundation for sorting through the Christian religions.

First before addressing the task of sorting out the Christian churches, two preliminary points must be addressed. As already noted human persons as far back in time as we can go have always behaved badly. At the present moment they continue to behave badly. God created an evolutionary world and prefers that world. God does not wave a magic wand but encourages slow change. Christianity is a leaven in our cultural evolution and indeed in our individual growth.

That evolutionary development also is part of the history of Christianity. The Gospels do not portray the followers of Jesus, his apostles and disciples, as spiritual superheroes. They are flawed, imperfect persons who develop over time sometimes as after the resurrection in sudden spurts. Christians ever since have been flawed and imperfect but in the process of change. The Christian Church is designed for sinners.

One reason for the divisions in Christianity is that Christians are sinners and have engaged in bad behavior. That is a fair description of some portions of Christian history and some aspects of present Christianity. That description applies to all the Christian churches including my own.

God, as the old saying goes, hates sin but loves the sinner. Jesus forgave and continues to forgive sinners. God puts up with but seeks to change our sinful behaviors. He accepts and deals with human nature where and as it is although He seeks to transform it. That is apparent throughout the Hebrew and Christian Bibles.

The division between the Churches is contrary to God's desires. Jesus prayed that we all may be one. Nevertheless God is prepared to use the various Churches and indeed other religions to promote His goals for human evolution, to act as a leaven in the world.

Second we should discuss the Eucharist. On the night before he died Jesus ate a Passover supper with His disciples. The Passover meal is one of the major festivals of the Jewish religion and commemorates the Exodus from Egypt and indeed the entire history of Israel and its relation with a Providential God. In the course of Passover Supper Jesus instituted the Eucharist.

Before going to church on Holy Thursday, the day before Good Friday when we remember Jesus' death on the Cross, my family and I eat what we call a Christian Passover Meal. We follow generally the format for a Jewish Passover Meal. In memory of the departure from Egypt and its hardships the bread at Passover is unleavened, currently Matzo. In the readings during the meal this unleavened bread is described as "the bread of affliction which our fathers ate in the desert." Addressing his disciples Jesus transformed this bread into His Body saying "Take this and eat it. This is My body which shall be given up for you". Again in the course of the meal at the time of the cup of blessing, the third of the four cups of wine poured during the supper, Jesus transformed the wine into His

Blood, saying "This is My Blood, the Blood of the new and everlasting covenant which will be shed for you so that sins may be forgiven." In the highest interpretation of this event Jesus transformed the bread of affliction into His Body and the cup of blessing into His Blood. He directed His disciples to do this in memory of Him.

Looked at historically Jesus at the Passover Meal provided the central rite for the religion His followers will carry to the world. He is continuing but transforming the Passover Meal. He is continuing the history of Israel but setting aside the Temple sacrifices and substituting this new rite, a reenactment and memory of His sacrifice on the Cross. You should refer here to the previous discussion of the sacrifice of Jesus. The memory of that sacrifice is to be the central rite of Jesus' transformation of the religion of Israel as He extends the blessings of Abraham to the gentiles.

In the context of the history of Israel, a history of a people wrestling with God, of God molding His people and dwelling with them in the cloud, the pillar of fire, the tent, the Ark of the Covenant and the Temple, Jesus is providing an obvious and concrete means by which He could continue to dwell with His people, to be Emmanuel, God with us, with each and every one of us who eat His Body and drink His Blood.

We have discussed above the question of whether this is an objectionable human sacrifice. That discussion should be incorporated here. We also have discussed the problem of miracles. I see no difficulty in God performing occasional or even regular miracles. In the modern world of science with evolution, random mutation, the uncertainty principle, there is amble room for divine intervention without disturbing the statistical regularities of the universe. Regularly transforming the bread and wine into His body and blood may offend scientific sensibilities but does not interfere with science.

Over the history of Christianity there has been much theological discussion of the ways and means and appropriate understanding of the transformation of the bread and wine into the Body and Blood of Jesus. I would just note that none of that discussion has accounted for something God knew over the ages but which we have just discovered, namely DNA. I will leave that as a teaser for you to play with. Think spiritual DNA.

In view of the history of Israel and the story of Christianity, a history and story of God with us, I would opt for the highest interpretation of this central rite of Christianity. This is the Body and Blood of Christ. This is God with us.

The most ancient of the Christian religions have always recognized that and still recognize it. In sorting out the Christian religions that would be an important touchstone. Do they take seriously the presence of God with us and this central rite of the Christian religion?

Ecumenicism

In view of Jesus' prayer that we may all be one, there is a serious basis for the modern practice of ecumenicism. As a people for whom Jesus died and whom He commanded to love one another we should at least talk to each other. Each of us is a child of God and deserving of deep respect and concern. Our fellow Christians of whatever denomination are our brothers and sisters in Christ. We can learn more about God and His Christ from conversing with each other and praying together.

I would apply that understanding to all religions certainly to all the religions descended from Abraham but also beyond that. I would find the presence of God in all religions. Jesus the Christ became human to become one of us. He died for each and every human person. He died not only for Christians or those of whatever particular denomination you favor but also for all including adherents of various pagan religions and those of no faith. Christians preserve the memory of Christ and provide the central vehicle for His continuing presence among us but Jesus identified with each and every one of us. Jesus identified with and ate with sinners and the non-religious. He surely is available to atheists and those of non-Christian religions in whatever way they and He can find to approach Him. One way is through doing good and loving others. Another is through prayer, even prayer to pagan gods. Prayer is a way of opening one's heart and mind to God.

Ecumenicism is vital; and respectful conversation in an effort to learn from others is necessary to following Christ. We must nevertheless choose among the Churches. The Lord Jesus came concretely in a time and place and directed His followers to preach the Gospel and follow specific central rites. He could have chosen to be an abstract, mystical God or even a providential God but not a God with us. Instead He chose the path of concrete love, hands on love. That will lead to concrete explicit religion. His followers are directed to love everyone. Christ identified with each of us. That requires respect for all religions. But nevertheless we must sort out the churches, however untactful that appears to modern consciousness. If we make a mistake, however, God will forgive us and continue to be with us.

Respectfully, I would suggest the ancient Christian churches as those most closely reflecting the basic message of Christ. This book, poems and essay, is written to support Christianity in general and to be helpful to all Christians. Obviously, however, I write for all from the perspective of my own religion, Roman Catholicism, to which I firmly adhere. Within the confines of this book, I don't propose to go further. Nevertheless, I sincerely recommend Roman Catholicism to you as meeting the criteria emerging from this discussion in a thorough going way.

Once you have made serious progress in sorting out the churches, you should take some concrete specific steps. You already may be a member of a church or your parents are. Staying with and seriously pursuing that church for a period of time makes great sense. Eventually you have to decide for yourself. In the course of that decision contact the pastor of a church or another member of the clergy. That cleric will welcome you and should prove helpful. If not, find another member of the clergy. In my own younger days a young assistant pastor at St. Peter's Church in Cambridge, Massachusetts, was extraordinarily helpful to me. I am eternally grateful to him.

Conclusion

In the poems and in this essay, I have provided you with a treasure map. I have skipped many questions, due to pressures of time and space. This essay is already too long. You must do further reading and thinking. I may have some of the coordinates wrong but I think I have correctly identified the island where the treasure lies and you will manage.

Recalling the Lord Jesus' discussion of treasure would be relevant here. There was a man, He narrated, who found a great treasure in a field, then reburied it and went and sold all he had and purchased that field. Again, He explained, the kingdom of heaven is like a man who found a pearl of great price and went and sold all he had and purchased that pearl. But what about the rest of us who have not done that? Jesus went forward in his parable now analogizing the kingdom of heaven to a great net. Or to put it in more colloquial terms, the Lord said we will get a great net and drag you all in and then sort out what is worthwhile. You and I with the help of God will probably be in that great net. But remember that the Lord Jesus also told us to seek to enter by the narrow way.

I have provided you with a treasure map. Use it well.

Thank you for reading this essay. Now go back and read the poetry again. Straight through. One volume each evening.

Post-script

I am, of course, not a trained theologian. I am an amateur legal philosopher and a voracious reader. As such I may have crossed the I's and dotted the t's. I may have gotten some of the coordinates on the treasure map wrong. I submit to the superior knowledge and judgment of those better trained and more wise than I. And I urge you to read further and discuss with those who understand religion better than I. But do search diligently and find that treasure.

Cited Books

Donnelly, Samuel, 2003, A Personalist Jurisprudence, The Next Step, Durham, Carolina Academic Press

Griffin-Jones, Robin, 2000, The Four Witnesses, San Francisco, Harper

Granfield, David 1988, The Inner Experience of Law, A Jurisprudence of Subjectivity, Washington, Catholic University

Heaney, Seamus, 1999, Opened Ground, Selected Poems 1966-1996, New York, Farrar, Straus and Giroux

Lonergan, Bernard, 1970, Insight: A Study of Human Understanding, New York, Philosophical Library

Lonergan, Bernard, 1973, Method in Theology, New York, Herder and Herder

Ratzinger, Joseph Cardinal (now Benedict XVI), 1969, 2004, An Introduction to Christianity, San Francisco, Communio Books, Ignatius Press

RatzInger, Joseph (Benedict XVI), 2007, Jesus of Nazareth, New York, Doubleday

Other Recommended Books

Martin, James 2007, My Life with the Saints, Chicago, Loyola Press

Merton, Thomas, 1998, 1948, The Seven Story Mountain, New York, Harcourt, Brace

Nouwen, Henri, 1992, The Return of the Prodigal Son, London, Darton, Longman and Todd

Nouwen, Henri, 1988, Road to Daybreak: A Spiritual Journal, New York, Doubleday

Ratzinger, Joseph (now Benedict XVI) 1998, In the Beginning, A Catholic Understanding of Creation and Fall, Grand Rapids, Eerdmans